Wavi

God is so prou
the woman you c
becoming. continue
to strive for Him,
and Him alone. He
will meet you right
where you are!

Love,

Before Saying "Yes" To The Ring

Things to consider before engagement: Inspired by
my story, scripture, letters, prayers, and poetry.

KAROLYNE ROBERTS

Published by IAMImage Limited Liability Company

If you would like to publish with us, or for information on special discounts or bulk orders of
Before Saying "Yes" to The Ring,
please email us at mail@iamimage.com

ISBN 978-1491050903

Scripture quotations are taken from the following versions: New International Version, New King James Version, King James Version.

Printed in the United States of America

Table of Contents

Acknowledgements

First and foremost I would like to dedicate this book to Daddy, my heavenly Father. Thank You so much for fighting for me. Thank You for showing me how precious I am and teaching me my worth. For always being by my side, and keeping Your promise of never leaving nor forsaking me, I love You.

I'd like to thank my husband, Chris, for always supporting me and believing in me. Thank you for dedicating our season of engagement to purity and celibacy and not treating me any less than I am worth.

Thank you Heather and Cornelius Lindsey for your ministries and bed checks! Thank you for dedicating so much time to counsel, support, and befriend Chris and I.

Damaris, I love you. Thank you for keeping me accountable, praying with me, and sticking by me through thick and thin. Thanks to everyone else who also held me accountable and to my friends Tiyahni, Christine, and Shaina, for being the best bridesmaids ever!

Last but certainly not least; I would like to thank my family for challenging me to be the best me that I can be. For their guidance, love, support, and prayers.

Foreword

I started an organization in 2012 called Pinky Promise. It is a promise to honor God with your life and your body and it's geared towards women. I started the organization because of my great struggle as a single. I chased after relationships in hopes that I would be made whole. After constantly coming up empty, I realized that only Christ could fill my many voids and that I needed him, not another boyfriend. Prior to starting the organization, I blogged towards women, encouraging them to honor God with their life and body and I shared my story of being whole, waiting to kiss until my wedding day and learning to trust God when I didn't understand. I travel on a weekly basis to speak at different states and I came across one of the sweetest women in Pinky Promise. Her name is Karolyne Roberts.

Since the very first time we met, she has been completely consistent. She's sweet, kind, and has such a pure heart. I first heard about her story when she and Chris had just gotten back together. I am so proud of their decision to be selfless and to honor God with their decision for a season.

I have watched Karolyne grow spiritually, emotionally, physically and just recently, into a wife! I am thrilled about her very first book and totally honored that she asked me to be a part of it. As you read this book, I pray that your heart is open and ready to be changed by the power of God's spirit. I believe that you picked this particular book for a reason and that God is going to minister to you right where you are. At times, we may pick up a book and read it for a little while and then put it down. I encourage you to read this book the entire way through and let God use it to meet you where you are in life.

Karolyne's story is a reminder to this generation that you can remain a virgin and honor God with your life though not "everybody" is doing it! This world tries to pressure you to do things that you don't have peace about and these temporary pleasures will never fulfill you. When you're in a relationship with someone and they want to "try you out"—just remember that you aren't a rental car. When a person rents out a car, they don't treat it as well if they were driving their own car. They push really hard on the gas & then break. They don't clean up after themselves, there's no sentimental value—because that car doesn't belong to the owner. Same thing happens when you're dating YOUR way versus God's way. That person is using you; they are breaking your heart, hurting you and not treating you like a precious jewel.

You see, woman—that man isn't committed to investing into your future. They're committed to temporarily leasing you out until they get tired of you and then they will return you back to the lot, used and broken. Before you get married, this book will help you to see your precious worth and value—so enjoy Before Saying "Yes" to The Ring.

Love,
Heather Lindsey
Founder, Pinky Promise
www.heatherllindsey.com

Part One

Introduction

This book was written to inform and bring to light the importance of preparing for the unique and very crucial season of engagement that is many times overshadowed by the hype over marriage. There are millions of books on what you need to do in order to be prepared for marriage or cope with singleness. Don't get me wrong: all are very helpful and purposeful, especially for people in the engagement stage. Still, what about those who have yet to encounter the process of engagement?

One day while I was sitting in my room, reflecting on my current relationship, which so happens to be my second engagement, I asked myself a few questions... "Did I rush into this?" "Was I ready to be engaged?" "What could I have done better?" I prayed for the answers, and I also researched my questions online. I was met with a ton of findings on marriage, though I clearly typed in "engagement" and nothing talked about how one can prepare or know if they're prepared for engagement. This book is my answered prayer from God. I got from Him the lessons I learned out of every circumstance during my engagement so that I can share it with you and even prepare myself thereafter for marriage.

Everyone talks about not rushing into marriage. Has anyone ever considered the fact that it is even possible to rush into engagement, or any season of life for that matter? I mean, do not get me wrong, realizing that I may have rushed did initially bring me some feelings of regret and insecurity, and that's all right.

It could not keep me down though, because I know the God that I serve and His word, which says, "And we know that all things work together for good to those who love God, to those who are the called according to His purpose." Romans 8:28 (New King James Version)

A little after the enemy tried to throw condemning thoughts into my head about my decision to get engaged at the time I did, I was reminded of this awesome truth. I was reminded that God has a purpose for me, for my life, and for all the decisions I have made in Him. I do not regret the place that I am at today. I have come to learn and grow so much from this experience, and now I am able to share what I have learned with you.

With that being said, this book is not only a sharing of my experiences and story with you, but a guide to help lead you into a faithful yet reasonable process of thought in deciding whether or not you are ready to either present or say yes to the big question: "Will you marry me?"

I am not writing a set of laws or demands, but simply inviting mere considerations that I hope will inspire you to prayerfully discern for yourself when your time is. From this, I hope that the singles really cherish and realize the richness that comes within their season, that the courting prepare for and wait for the process, and that the engaged commit to the process.

My Testimony

When I was younger, there was a little girl I would play with. She was the daughter of a family friend. One day, I had so much fun playing with the little girl that I didn't want to go home. I asked my mom if I could sleep over for just that one time, and I did. A few hours after my mom left, two of the little girls cousins came over. They were boys. One was older; a kid around the age of twelve, and the other one was our age. The older boy molested me. He said, "Lets play house" and insisted that he be the daddy and I be the mommy and the others would be the kids. I had never played house like this before, when I tried moving his hand away, he slapped it, and went on doing his thing.

That opened up doors in my life to a lot of things concerning sexual immorality. From that point on little girls came up to me, wanting to kiss me in the bathroom stall or put their hands under my skirt at the picnic table. This happened a few times. Then, I started having experiences with family members when we played house. I was young and confused.

As I got a little older, eventually I became exposed to pornography. I started masturbating, looking out for pornography, and many times specifically for lesbian porn. I would go to live sex chat rooms on the Internet and so on. In my eighth grade year I began talking to guys. I'd talk to multiple guys at the same time. I was always kissing the boys at my school and creating drama between me and other girls.

I was so desperate to be in a relationship. I was desperate for attention from men. Now, I know who my Father is, God, in whom I've found everything I've ever desired and more. He has shown me my worth and is the closest thing to me. I thank God for restoring me. I was able to keep my virginity and honor my husband with it on our wedding day. This is because throughout all my life, though I was wrapped up in different relationships, God kept calling me back to Him. He also placed a deep conviction in me, which has always stopped me from fully turning away from the Truth I grew up in.

Today I am a woman who has been delivered from the bonds of sexual immorality. I am no longer addicted to pornography and neither do I struggle with homosexual thoughts. Now I counsel other women on how to break free from these addictions and combat homosexuality as well as pursuing purity.

My Story: The Movies

Did you know that Satan answers prayers too? He answers prayers that he knows are not in God's will, but can manipulate and use them to have you justify every sinful place that he wants to take you. At fourteen years old I had already written my list of what I wanted in a guy. Some of the first things I ever wanted were:

- Someone light-skinned with dreads

- Someone who had a lot of muscles

- Someone who was a "Christian"

The items on that list are a direct reflection of my naïveté during that season. When I said I wanted a "Christian," I just meant I wanted someone who went to church. I know now that going to church alone does not make you a true Christian. Having a relationship with Jesus and exemplifying Christ-likeness does.

I had the type of mindset that had not been renewed and pictured God as Santa Claus. I thought I could go to Him to have all my little selfish desires fulfilled. Many people get stuck in this mindset because when they have received what they have asked for, they credit God and count it as an answered prayer from Him, when many times He has nothing to do with it. This mindset is what bound me to relationships that I knew dishonored God, while using Him as the excuse for my actions.

That person that you keep sinning with, are you sure that that's who God has for you? That person who is constantly drawing you away from Him, are they really an "angel," only because they are supporting you financially? Have you become a slave to them because you are scared that if you let go, God won't bring you anything better? Don't be fooled into thinking that your bondage to someone is dedication; once you make something your God, you become a slave to it, and now it has the control, not you.

One night I went to a movie theater with my best friend Tiyahni. I laid eyes on a guy that I determined in my heart would be mine. The pursuit began with me going to the concession stand and buying candy that I could eat seductively as I walked across the arcade trying to snatch his attention. I swayed my hips dramatically from left to right and drenched my lips with Victoria's Secret lip-gloss, my secret weapon of the time. Despite all my efforts and failed attempts of luring in his attention, I tried again after seeing this boy at the movies only a few weeks later. He never paid me any mind.

Yet in my head I began to believe that it was meant to be. There was no way that I could see this guy a second time at the movies and not think it was fate. You could see my selfish desires and a deep hope that God would answer my prayer for a husband in action. The boy had fit many of the descriptions that I had wanted, and I really believed that with God on my side, and just a little manipulation, I could have him!

He was tall, was light-skinned, had dreads, and had muscles. All of those shallow terms had been a part of my silly little list. The only almost reasonable thing that I asked for was that he be a Christian. I say "almost reasonable" because the very fact that I added Christianity and faith into my whole selfish mix made it all the more absurd. Later on I would take the fact that he claimed Christianity as justification for my relationship with him. I would manipulate further and further and try to change him, to try to get his lifestyle to line up with his words and my desires.

The third time I saw him was at the library. I had hoped that at that moment he would notice me. He was with two of his cousins, who had also been with him when I saw him at the movies previously. While at the library, we all had been sitting in the same computer section, and to my surprise, his cousins came over and tried to "holler at me." I could not even focus on what they were saying. I was too busy wondering why he still wasn't paying any attention to me. Watching him over by the computer, minding his own business, made me want him more. Obviously this was not "fate": I was just pushing to make something happen that clearly was not meant to be.

Eventually they ended up leaving the section of the library that we were in. Then when I finally gained the confidence to talk to him, he was gone. I ran frantically through every single aisle in the library and could not find him! I was devastated when I realized that I had let him go for a third time, and I promised myself that if I ever came across him again, I would tell him everything and never let him go. Talk about being a stalker!

One day one of my friends and I were having a sleepover, and I told her about the list I wrote, my story, and how I felt this guy was "the one." While we were talking, she was on the computer after having reactivated her MySpace account, and I told her to put me back on her top ten friends list. While looking through her friends list to find me, she skimmed across a picture that looked like the guy. I jumped and said, "Wait! I think that's him; click that picture!" We were taken to his page, and we saw that it was he, the guy that I had just been telling her about. I asked her how she knew him, and she said she did not know him that well, but she believed he went to a high school that she was thinking of going to. We were in the eighth grade at the time.

After being made aware of my secret lover's presence on social media, I logged on to my own MySpace account and sent him a friend request. When he accepted it, I sent him a long message of my story, and it started off with something along the lines of, "I know this may sound weird but..." From there we began speaking casually on MySpace for a few days. I don't think he trusted me to have his number yet!

Shortly after that, one evening Tiyahni and I went to the movies to watch Tyler Perry's recent movie at the time, called Why Did I Get Married? I loved the movie so much! My aunt was in town the next week from Jamaica, and she was not used to going out to the movies, so my Grandma and I wanted to do something fun with her. I had recommended that we all go watch the movie. A while after we had made plans to go to the movies later that evening, I went on to the computer to check my MySpace account. I got a message from the guy answering my previous question, "What are you doing today?" He replied saying that he would be going to the movies with his cousins. I told him that I was going to the movies too, with my grandmother and aunt.

When we got there, it turned out that the movie was sold out. When my Grandma asked whether there was another theater we should go to, I requested that we go to the one I usually went to with Tiyahni. It was only a natural response, but shortly after, I remembered that the guy was going to the movies, and I began to panic! "OH MY GOSH, OH MY GOSH, OH MY GOSH," I began to proclaim in the car on the way there. My grandma and aunt asked me what all the drama was about, and I explained to them my story. They thought I was just being a dramatic teenager.

While we sat in the back of the theater, watching the previews, I followed after the guy and his cousins as they walked past us to their seats. I sat right next to the guy and said, "Hey, it's Karolyne from MySpace." He took his phone and shined it in my face, and he said, "Oh... Hi, I'm Chico." We sat there awkwardly for three minutes, and my grandma came over to us and said, "Karolyne, come to your seat." I was kind of annoyed by that, but she meant the best. I told him sorry, that I had to go and would message him on MySpace when I got home.

As soon as I got back home from the movies, I messaged him. He told me he was getting ready for bed and finally gave me his number. The rest was history. Every day after that, we talked on the phone for hours. He made me tell him the story again and I convinced him that God had orchestrated the whole thing. He told me he was a Christian and a story about how he got the scar on his face, how he was attacked by a Rottweiler and believed in God because when he was in the ambulance he saw angels standing there with him. That incident is what gave him faith. I then decided that I wanted to help him grow his faith and move him closer to God. Little did I know, I needed to be moved closer to God myself.

I ended up breaking up with the boyfriend that I had at the time. I had been dating someone who was talking about marrying me while all this was going on. I knew he was still messing with his ex-girlfriend, and I did not take his comments about wanting to "wife me" seriously.

Chico and I eventually planned a day where we could actually hang out in person for the first time. We said that we would meet at the library. I lied to my mom and told her I had a late-night, last-minute project to do, and she dropped me off. I was on the phone with him, walking to the place where we had planned to meet, under the tent outside. It was around 6:00 or 7:00 p.m. Later on in our relationship he would go on to tell me that the first time he saw me, there was a glow all around me and that's how he knew I was the one. We were both dramatic. Supposedly I walked into the tent with my glow and found him sitting on the picnic table. We held hands and walked around the community college library, and when we got near a metal fence, he leaned me against it, and as the wind blew softly through my fake weave, he kissed me and I felt like, "Yes, this is the fairy tale that I always wanted! Like in a movie! Thank You, Jesus!"

Soon after that, life got real and my fairytale I manipulated together began to look more like prison than anything else. Eventually my mom caught on to my lies of having to go to the library and work on projects, and one day she let me walk in, stayed in the parking lot, and shortly after watched me walk out with Chico. That was the first time that she met him. She gave us a speech about not lying and about being open and real if we wanted to date. My birthday was coming up, and I asked my mom if he could take me out to dinner, she said yes and he did. He bought me flowers, a teddy bear, and a card, and it felt like prom. His mom was there, and he opened the car door for me and was so polite. He was really "falling in love" with me.

Now when I look back, I am so sorry for all the emotional ups and downs that I put him through. My tactics did not lead him closer to God; if anything, they led him further away, and they led me further away as well. He was loyal and a sweetheart. He had the talent of singing and playing the piano. He had some faith, but I began to judge him. I found out about his involvement in drugs and gangs. I hated that he was a rapper, and while we were dating, his lyrics seemed to be getting more secular over time. I only liked it when he rapped about me.

I was such a hypocrite. I tried weed, would sneak to see him, and though I was determined to keep my virginity, had shameful sexual conversations with him over the phone and sent him degrading pictures of myself that caused him to lose respect for me and lust even more after me. Our relationship was very rocky, and we were on and off for months, mainly because of my confusion between him being the one and trying to make him the one at the same time. We were on and off because something about him could never fully satisfy me, but something else in me wanted to manipulate him into doing so. He was like a project that I was working on fixing for my own selfish desires. Eventually he began feeling suicidal because he was tired of me coming in and out of his life. He would make threats that if I left him again, he would kill himself.

I remember one night wanting to break up with him so bad and he felt it. He was sitting on top of a roof while on the phone with me, and he told me that if I broke up with him, he'd jump. I wanted to break up with him because I could no longer take the disrespect. He started changing throughout our relationship, and I suffered the emotional abuse of being called out of my name, being belittled, and controlled. I felt trapped. I felt empty too.

Then, on the fourth of July, before my tenth-grade year in high school, I had a breakdown and went into prayer. I cried out to God. I repented for all that I had done in the relationship, and I told Him I felt trapped and scared. What I had begun to control was taken out of my control. I realized the truth of my doings and that God had nothing to do with it. I asked Him to please take Chico out of my life somehow, and I told Him that I would dedicate myself to getting to know Him. I went to bed in tears, just hoping that God would make a way.

The next morning Chico called me and said he had a weird dream. When I asked him what the dream was, he told me that it was of us breaking up. I told him, "Maybe this is a sign from God," and he said, "Yeah." At that moment we were no longer together. He had agreed so smoothly, and I hung up and was at peace.

My Story: The Show

Entering into my tenth-grade year, I had a new heart and desire to serve God. Around the same time I began going to a new church that had been teaching the word of God like I'd never heard before. I started to read my bible more and grew in a deeper knowledge of God. Little by little, my life started to change.

During my time with Chico, I had grown close to a boy that I met back in the eighth grade. We became good friends because I moved into a new neighborhood where he lived really close to me. From that moment on we'd always be at each other's houses, walking around the neighborhood, going to the park, eating at the nearest pizzeria, and so on.

He became my "best friend" even though I had previously had a crush on him before even having met Chico. He was there for me and listened to me and gave the best advice when Chico and I would get into arguments or when I was feeling depressed.

Our close relationship continued and even began to grow after Chico and I broke up. I grew close to his family, and he grew close to mine. All the while, this was around the time that I was growing closer to God as well, because of the new church I had joined.

I also started to attend a bible study group at my high school called "First Priority," and people started to look at me differently and began to recognize my newfound love for God's word. Soon I was elected President of the club. That scared me. Even though I was growing in God, I could not forget all the wrong that I had done in my previous relationship with Chico. It felt wrong to be the President of the Christian club at school. Everyone was looking up to me and asking me for prayer and advice while at the same time I was struggling with my own demons. I had an addiction to pornography and used to masturbate due to my past of being molested and previous homosexual experiences at such a young age. I was not ready to be put on the pedestal. I had been growing closer to God, but I still needed deliverance in many areas.

After a few weeks of gathering sermons together and preaching them to the students at my school, I resigned. I felt like those sermons were for me more than for those I was preaching to. It was the first time I was really learning and reading from the bible. Still, my heart turned towards other things that I thought would be able to quench my thirst.

I was like the Pharisee to which the bible says in Mathew 15:8 (New International Version), "These people honor me with their lips, but their hearts are far from me." Breaking up with Chico was the opportunity I had to really turn my life around and totally chase after God, but I got distracted quickly. I began the course, but did not keep it. As Galatians 5:7 (New International Version) says, "You were running a good race, who cut in on you to keep you from obeying the truth?"

Eventually my emotional feelings for my "best friend" that I had back in middle school returned. I was single and became jealous of him always talking to me about his ex-girlfriend or new girls he had been talking to. I never got jealous when he would speak about girls before. It was normal for us to talk about our significant others, but for the first time, I did not have one. Chico was the first guy that I did not have sidelines or backups for because I thought he was my first true love. He had talked about marrying me and us moving into his parents' house to live. I was crazy for even agreeing with the plan. I do not think God's plan for me is to get married to anyone whose plan is to move in with them and their parents. We were young and naïve all right!

One day after my "best friend" showed me pictures of this new girl he was talking to, I got emotional. Later that day, his mom had sent us to do some grocery shopping at Publix. Shopping in the grocery store with him made me look at him as a husband. When I asked him how he felt about what we were doing (we were just simply shopping at the grocery store), he had no idea what I was talking about and I got so frustrated and mad! He was so confused!

Later that night I called him on the phone all mad. I got on him about all the girls he was talking to and how he didn't even feel anything at the grocery store and how I felt different all of a sudden. I told him I loved him. I am sure he must have been overwhelmed from hearing all of that. By that time we had known each other for three years, been "best friends" for two, and had previously dated for about a week during one summer while I was in New York. A few days after my dramatic phone call to him, he texted his feelings to me, told me that he loved me, and asked me to be his girlfriend. I said yes. That was in April of 2010.

From then on we became a popular couple among the people in our network of high school kids after moving on from being the "celebrity best friends." When I tell you EVERYONE knew about our relationship, I mean EVERYONE. That kind of annoyed me. I did not like how he would post about me on Facebook all the time. I do not like people in my business, unless I'm writing a book, of course.

We created this glorified image of ourselves through social media. Everyone thought we were the perfect couple. He was smooth with his words, very charming, a guy with good character. I was smart, sweet, and talented, so they say. Everyone looked at us this way. I think people idolized our relationship just as much as we did. We became concerned with presenting ourselves in a certain light. Like everything was perfect and we loved each other so much. Again on a pedestal, we were destined to fall.

Eventually he proposed to me on April 15, 2011, which was exactly a year since we had been dating. I said yes. I was so excited to finally be a step closer to the dream that I've always wanted. I thought, "Yes, thank you God! I am so blessed!"

Soon, our faithfulness to God began to grow sour, and it came back to bite us. Our relationship ended due to an issue of unfaithfulness. The bible says in Galatians 6:7 (King James Version), "Be not deceived; God is not mocked: for whatsoever a man soweth, that shall he also reap."

One day in June of 2011, I got a phone call in the middle of the night. Three months after my ex had asked me to be his wife, I found out that revealing pictures of him were exposed on social media, which were found in the phone of his new "best friend," from her boyfriend. The sad part about it is, a few days before that, he had sent me those same pictures to my phone, and told me that it was only for my eyes to see, his future wife. Come to find out that was a lie.

I was supposed to leave for college the day that I found out, but I had previously decided to stay one more day because I wanted to be there for his birthday. Instead, I ended up breaking up with him on his birthday. I was infuriated and so hurt! I had never been cheated on before, and for the first time I got a little hint of how God maybe feels when we chase after idols and forget Him. Revelation 2:4 (New International Version), "Yet I hold this against you: you have forsaken the love you had first." Before all of this happened, we were being unfaithful towards God. Leading up to that moment were other moments in which I was alone with him, trying to seduce him, trying to push the buttons without going all the way. I've got to say, when it came to sexual immorality within our relationship, I was the initiator most of the time. For the most part, my ex was respectful of the boundaries we wanted to keep, but I was the one who disrespected those boundaries.

I thought my engagement meant that I was blessed—but really? Blessed for not honoring God? Blessed for putting Him on the backburner and creating my own idols? Yes, God is faithful even when we are not, but He had nothing to do with this. It was all me manipulating to get closer to what I wanted. I cursed myself. Like it says in Deuteronomy 11:26–28 (New International Version), "See, I am setting before you today a blessing and a curse—the blessing if you obey the commands of the LORD your God that I am giving you today; the curse if you disobey the commands of the LORD your God and turn from the way that I command you today by following other gods, which you have not known."

I was worshiping the thought and desire of getting married, and I was cursed. The end of my relationship was not only a result of this curse, but also thankfully a result of God's providence and intervention. For a second time, He turned me away from going down a path of destruction!

The timing was perfect. I was walking into my new season and leaving behind the past. The next day I was off to Tallahassee, Florida, for college, only approximately 8–9 hours' drive away from the pain, yet closer than ever to my deliverance.

The Best Proposal in History

I was proposed to
in a swap shop modie drive through.
I didn't know that I'd turn out to be
a drive through too
and that my ex
would turn around
and trade me for his next
so I called that moment the best
moment of my life.
I thought I was ready to be a wife
to a man
that traded that moment
for the girl he called his best friend.
I had the lowest self-esteem.
I couldn't imagine that God would want
anything better for me,
I didn't have enough faith
so I settled for a dream.
But eventually I had to face
the nasty reality
and I thank God that He woke me
before the fall,
because that summer
He shinned light through it all.
On all the lies and pretending,
a love that was so fake.
Jesus got me out

before it was too late
because in June 2011
we could no longer defend us
because my ex and his best friend
helped end us.
Loyalty and trust
went out the window
leaving us vulnerable
 to insecurities and little devils.
It's funny how sin duplicates
and spreads like a cancer
and it can lead to destruction
if you don't find the answer.
If you don't find the cure
in the midst of everything
so obscure, like the cells in our bodies
selling out
will soon bring disease.
I left God on the back burner
and I started attracting fleas
because I didn't think
He was good enough for me.
Even though He saved me
from that relationship before the fall
when the fall came I started falling
because I continued following
after everything my heart desired
and never took the time to desire
the One who pulled me out of the fire.

I was a freshman in college
trying everything wrong
cause I was so desperate to find the one
not realizing that I wasn't even one yet.
I wasn't whole but broken,
because I didn't guard my heart
so it got stolen
with my consent.
So I tried to bring my past
into my present
by messing around with my ex-s'
little mini me's
but neglecting the present of God's presence
patiently waiting for me
so faithfully.
My life had always been
a lifestyle of idolatry
because even though God said,
"you shall have no other God's before me"
My relationships always took
first priority.
So I never let God have
authority over my life
What I chose to do with my own free will
brought me all the pain and the strife.
I went to church, knew God's will,
and understood what He liked
and didn't like
but I still

disobeyed Him

because I said my life was mine.

I was sinning yet praying,

feeding my flesh yet praising,

behind closed doors indulging

in sexual immorality while justifying everything

with my own doctrine

and un-renewed mentality.

I wasn't faithful to God

but I wanted my ex

to be faithful to me.

But God saved me

from making the biggest

mistake of my life.

No, not from marrying a guy who

would have more than one wife.

But from living a life without experiencing

the life-changing and healing power

of the Love of Christ.

He helped me get back my soul.

Healed me,

and made me whole.

All of me is right here, in Him.

Where I should have been

Before I even thought of

committing to the Lord.

Now any man that wants my hand

needs to go through Him.

I'm not sharing my identity

with someone who ain't washed of sin.
I'm not spreading the curse
to the next generation,
and if I have to I'll live a life
of full consecration till the end.
God will determine my final destination.
Jesus is the author
and finisher of my salvation
I trust in Him.
I have no further obligations
but to trust Him
so I won't rush Him.
I will continue to touch the hem
of His garment
so that His healing power could rush in.
Enough is enough and it's in Him--No
He's more than enough
I'm always content and satisfied.
Sex, money, and love from men
won't quench my appetite.
My spirit is thirsty
and if a man can't feed me spiritually,
He has nothing to offer me.
So the next time a man asks me to marry him
I should not need to ask why.
he should be a manifestation of the Father
he should remind me of Christ.
he should know that we're the bride
before I am his

because Christ is the first reason
that we all have to live.
He died for us,
laid down His life for us,
the best proposal in history--
the bible even calls it a mystery.
Will you accept it?
Will you accept Him?
Will you, say "yes"?

My Story: The Transition

I had a heart issue. That is what made me unclean. It eventually showed through my actions, and my life finally began to line up with what was going on inside of me. You cannot play the role of goody-two-shoes for too long. Eventually the truth will come to light. Eventually your true colors will show and you will be revealed as the hypocrite you are.

Now, whether you use that revelation as an opportunity to change and testify of God's grace and goodness, or whether you use that revelation as an opportunity to sulk in condemnation and continue down that path, is up to you. I chose to turn my past into a testimony instead of making it my life story.

When I got to college I met some guys on campus who became my fellow mentors. They were starting a photography business called Ringside Entertainment and Productions (REP), and the CEO of the business, Ecclesiast, was also a former president of an organization on campus called "Poetic Lyricism."

Back in high school I had gotten into spoken-word poetry and was also doing my freelance photography business on the side. I thought working with REP would be the perfect opportunity to develop and utilize my creative gifts. Ecclesiast ("Cle"), Lawrence, and Jephte took my newfound friend Damaris and me under their wings. Because of them we got unique opportunities to photograph with people like Cornel West, the Wayans Brothers, and Maya Angelou. They were also there to give us advice, direction, and incredible friendship.

I joined Poetic Lyricism even before having met Cle. Before moving to college, I had contacted the current president at the time on Facebook and secured an e-board position as the historian for the organization. I was also involved in the Black Student Union's Nubian Waves magazine.

I attended one of Poetic Lyricism's open-mic nights at a spot called The Warehouse to support all of the poets who were performing. My now husband, Chris, was also there. In fact, that is where I met him. He and his friends had a daiquiri business and had been co-hosting the event. I love virgin strawberry daiquiris to this day!

Around that time, though I had broken up with my ex, we had been still talking and trying to figure things out. A few days before that open-mic event, though, I was on the phone with my ex and he was telling me that maybe we should try seeing other people and then see whether we still wanted to be with each other or not. I got so mad when he came up with such a scheme! Even though I broke up with him for cheating, part of me was insecure, did not think I could find anyone better, was scared, and still wanted to be with him. I told him, "No, I'm not interested in anyone else but you. You're the one I love!" Still, he kept insisting that we date other people. So out of spite and anger, I started talking to a lot of guys to entertain my madness and hurt.

When I met Chris at the open-mic night, I had been stringing along three other guys, guys who I really had no interest in and with whom I knew the relationship wouldn't be going anywhere, but I was just angry at my ex so I dated them.

That night I went to the bar and in a flirty voice asked Chris if I could have a free drink. At the end of the night, he came up to me and asked for my number. That's how I met him. To this day when we tell our story, he likes to share the part about how, when right before I asked for a free drink, he had just finished lecturing his partners about how they needed to stop giving away free drinks or else they would make no money. Then he gave me one!

The next night Chris texted me while I was at a Black Student Union mixer. He then came there to chill with me, and we just sat and talked for a bit. I learned that he was Jamaican and Indian, and he learned I was Jamaican and Haitian. He was a senior at Florida A&M University for graphic design, and we shared other minor facts about ourselves.

The next night, he asked if he could come over to my apartment to chill. He bought over some cards, which played... and while we were lying on my bed I came at him with a lot of whammies that he was definitely not expecting to hear. I told him that I was a virgin and that I was not having sex with him and that I wanted to save my virginity for my husband. He thought I was a liar! Then when I told him that I was eighteen years old and just came to college, he really thought I was lying! I also told him that I just got out of an engagement, and he was shocked. I asked him if he went to church and told him I was a Christian; he said no. Obviously I was giving off the wrong impression, but we had two different mindsets anyways. Chris thought I was totally someone else when he asked for my number. He had no idea what he was getting himself into.

Chris started coming over almost every night after that, and it started getting hard to hide him from my ex. My ex and I used to videoconference and text almost every night, and I didn't want him to know about Chris. I started to really like Chris, and the other guys who I had been stringing along—I just began ignoring them and blowing them off, and eventually they got the point.

It began with him leaving late at night, and then ended up with him sleeping over because one night he made the excuse, "My lights are out at the crib, can I sleep here?" and he continued making that excuse every night. It became normal for him to sleep over. We did not have sex. We literally just kissed and slept in the bed with his arms wrapped around me. I just loved the feeling of having a strong man to hug me to sleep.

I loved it when he would come over with food and say, "Honey, I'm home," and then we'd watch a movie and fall asleep together. Plus, he'd drive me to school the next morning, and I enjoyed not having to take the bus.

One night while videoconferencing with my ex, he began to catch on. He had a feeling that I had started seeing someone, and at that moment, I got a text from Chris that startled me! Chris needed a place to stay, and he asked me if I could be there for him. There was something different about that text. I was so worried. I hysterically told my ex, "I've got to go," and he was like, "Why? What's going on?" and I was like, "Nothing, I'll tell you later, bye." Minutes later Chris was banging on my door, drunk as can be, stumbling over; my heart was broken to see him like this.

He started throwing up; I cleaned up what hadn't made it into the toilet, took off his shoes, and tucked him in bed. I then used my voice to soothe him to sleep. "Just rest, baby. It's ok. Just rest," and eventually he fell asleep. I prayed for him. I laid out some sheets to sleep on the floor and woke up the next morning while he was still asleep so that he wouldn't know I had slept on the floor. It wasn't until a few weeks later when I told him I had slept on the floor because I didn't want him to feel bad. At that moment, I was wondering—wondering what that nurturing spirit was and where it came from. I realized that I really liked him.

One day while I was on Facebook, I saw that one of my friends posted a link to a blog on my page, a blog written by Heather Lindsey, the Founder and CEO of Pinky Promise, which is an organization that promotes purity amongst women and a vow to honor God with their bodies and lives. I followed the link and was blown away by what I read on her blog! Reading her story about her and her husband and how they waited until their wedding day to kiss really struck me. I had never heard anything like that before. I started to follow her and her husband's ministry and I learned so much from their messages on singleness, courting, and the purpose of marriage. My whole mindset began to transform, and I started seeing myself differently as well as seeing things differently regarding relationships.

I remember, one night after having started following Heather and Cornelius Lindsey's ministry online, I was lying in bed about to go to sleep in Chris's arms, and I heard the Holy Spirit whisper, "You don't need a man to keep you warm at night." My heart jumped! I felt so convicted! After that night, our relationship would never be the same. I started growing a conscience and was being built up in my inner man, also known as the Holy Spirit. This is what the bible says about the Holy Spirit in John 16:13 (New International Version): "But when he, the Spirit of truth, comes, he will guide you into all the truth. He will not speak on his own; he will speak only what he hears, and he will tell you what is yet to come." Since I began hearing from the Holy Spirit, it was harder to do what I knew was displeasing to God.

One day, I asked Chris out to a restaurant called Chipotle so that we could have a talk. That night we went to Chipotle and we sat down as I presented my new standards and rules that I wanted him to respect and abide by. I told him, "You're not my boyfriend; you haven't earned the right to kiss me, or to sleep over at my house, or to come over at all... from now on, you're not allowed to kiss me or come into my house because I respect myself and I have standards."

He was blown away and in complete shock and confusion! First of all, to him, this came out of nowhere. Secondly, he did not understand what this meant or why I was doing this. He was like, "What friends have you been talking to? What made you decide this all of a sudden? What things have you been listening to?" I responded, "Nothing! I just realize that I should have standards and respect myself."

He wasn't having it. He refused to do this no-kissing thing because we had already been kissing. We sat there for about an hour arguing over it. Then we made a deal. Before that meeting I had been begging him for a while to do a bible study with me. Especially because one time when I had a conversation with him about Christianity he said that he would never set foot in a church. Now at Chipotle he sat there in front of me and said, "I will do a bible study with you if you give me one more kiss." At the time I compromised and gave him one more kiss at the end of the night.

At that moment I thought that compromising was worth getting him to do a bible study, but God prefers obedience to sacrifice. It says in 1st Samuel 15:22 (New International Version), "But Samuel replied: 'Does the LORD delight in burnt offerings and sacrifices as much as obeying the LORD? To obey is better than sacrifice, and to heed is better than the fat of rams.'" The form of compromising would continue throughout my future interactions with Chris, and I would eventually learn how dangerous it was. Who was I kidding? I can't seduce someone to salvation!

A week later we met for our first bible study together at my school library. I ended up showing him a lot of convicting poetry videos from the Passion for Christ Movement as well as some videos about the illuminati, etc. It really shook him because at that time he had been listening to a lot of rap and his favorite rapper was J. Cole. I guess I wanted to start our first bible study somewhere where I would not feel like a hypocrite, because I had been resenting secular music for a while. I still listened to old-school jams and some contemporary things, but it seemed like a good place to start.

He loved the bible study and agreed to continue them with me. As we started growing together, he began to grow fonder of me and even began to change and draw closer to Christ. He respected me more and began doing things that he never did. He started taking me out to dinner and opening doors for me. Before, when we had been messing around, he'd never take me out. He would just come to my house, make out with me, sleep in my bed, and drop me to school the next day as a courtesy.

Even then I would feel a little insecure about our casual and non-committed relationship. I used to always say things like, "How come you never take me out on a date? You just come over to my house," and he would tell me how I am not his girlfriend and we're not at that level yet. I'd be thinking, "What! So we are at the level for you to kiss up on me and sleep in my bed, but not at the level to be committed to each other?" What he was really saying was, "I have no respect for you, so there's no point in dating you." Initially, he did not have the intention of possibly remaining committed to me in the long run.

Now, for the first time, I felt like Chris really liked me. At one of our dinner dates at this Chinese restaurant, it was made clear that we both saw that our relationship could turn into something serious. I don't remember his exact words, but I remember Chris talking to me and saying something along the lines of, "I know what I want," and that stuck with me. I knew he wanted me, to be with me, and that he was going to work at getting to that point.

Even though he wasn't my boyfriend yet, he was taking me out on dates. Before we had the conversation in Chipotle about standards and rules, I remember one night he was over at my apartment, the fact that I was still talking to my ex came up. I don't recall how it did—he may have seen messages from my ex in my phone. Regardless of what gave it away, he gave me an ultimatum. "Choose," he said. "You either be with your ex, or you let go of your past and be with me."

Clearly Chris was not up for sharing, even if I wasn't his girlfriend. Yet even then, I saw something in him. Or maybe I'm just being dramatic. Maybe it was his eight-pack that was all up in my face that I could not get over! Anyway, I told him that I definitely wanted him, and I wrote a long breakup message to my ex in front of him to prove it. The message basically said that I was done with the relationship and I was ready to move on.

That crushed my ex because we were in the middle of trying to work it out. Not to mention he was a rapper and had just finished releasing about four tracks on the Internet dedicated to me. His lyrics expressed how much he "loved" me and about how he was sorry for what happened and that he still wanted to be with me if I could just forgive him. Yet he was nine hours away, and Chris was right there in my bed, next to me. He was the one who would hug me at night, so it seemed so much easier to let go of a relationship and friendship that I had worked to build over the past five years.

Before this, I had just learned about "Soul Ties" by listening to Justin Cox, the founder of the Passion for Christ Movement, and I realized that a soul tie was definitely something that I had with my ex. My soul was intertwined with his, and it was so hard to let him go. Soul ties usually happen through sex, but can also happen when you are deeply intimate with someone. My ex and I were so close. We would be on the phone 24/7. We shared everything—of course except the things we were hiding. Our level of intimacy had developed over the years, and it followed me to Tallahassee. Though we broke up before I left, it was like I could not get rid of him. Everything around me reminded me of him. Besides the mix tape that I had that he made for me and the fact that I'd play it over millions of times in my room, almost every shoe, piece of jewelry, article of clothing, notebook, and diary was from him, about him, or brought back memories of him.

That is how it looks when your relationship turns into your God. It completely consumes your entire life! I did a lot of research on soul ties and what it takes to break them. It led to a confession ceremony that I orchestrated in my room in which I renounced my soul tie to my ex and I took all the stuff that he ever gave me and things that reminded me of him and put them in a big garbage bag and into my apartment complex's dumpster. Still, there were some things that were hard to throw away, like my engagement ring, my diaries that held special moments we shared, our prom portraits, etc. I put those in a separate garbage bag and took them to Cle and Lawrence's apartment.

The very act of keeping those things are symbolic of how some things in my heart were buried, but never fully dealt with and eventually resurfaced. It is easy to separate yourself from a thing, but when it's time to face it, that is when you know if you have truly overcome that thing or if you are still in bondage to it.

With that being said, let's go back to the time when Chris started dating and respecting me. Everything was going great, but then Christmas break came along and it was time for me to go back home for the holidays. The first person I visited while being back home was my ex. I got in my emotions and completely disregarded what was going on between Chris and I in Tallahassee. I began wanting my ex back and began hanging out with him every day. My ex was so hurt because he wanted to be with me, but he knew about Chris and he could not get over the message I sent him.

I was an emotional wreck who was only thinking of myself, and I hurt everyone else involved. On Christmas Eve, I remember sitting on the couch with my ex and having our legs wrapped together and taking a picture of it and posting it on Twitter.

That day I got a phone call from Chris, and I stepped away from my ex and picked up. Chris asked what I was doing, and I was giving him really vague, beat-around-the-bush type answers. Then he asked me about the picture. Chris had seen the picture online, and he was deeply hurt. All I could do was say sorry. I felt so dumb, caught, and mad. My whole mood was sour for the rest of the night even though my ex and I were at a family event.

After Chris hung up, I told my ex what happened as if he was wrong for doing it with me. He was like, "So? He will be fine." I was crazy out of my mind to expect my ex to be sympathetic of my actions towards Chris after everything I have put him through as well. That night I told my ex, "I don't want to be with you. I don't love you," and other mean things that really hurt him, and now come to think of it, I was a big part of why everything would fall out horribly later on like it did. It wasn't just him being "crazy" like I'd always tell the story. I moved him to that point.

I was on the phone with Chris, and I was like, "I am so sorry I hurt you! Please forgive me! I want to be with you. I don't want him. I told him that it's officially over. Please, you don't deserve this; you've been so good to me." He said he needed to pray about it. That was the first time I ever heard him say anything like that! I was a little shocked and even madder that it looked like I was about to lose a man who prayed. The following are the email messages between Chris and me that followed our initial phone conversation:

From: Karolyne Daudin

To: Christopher Roberts

Date: Sun, Dec 25, 2011 at 6:20 pm

"You had every right to lose trust in me. If you were to trust me now, you'd only be trusting in the God that's in me and the influence He has on who I am as a person. But, you have to choose if you want to take the risk of giving me a chance... a chance to earn your trust for who I am as Karolyne the human.

If I were you, I'd only take a risk on something that was worth it. Something that has potential... kind of like the potential I saw in you. And thank you for exceeding my expectations.

Is the Karolyne that you got to know over these past few months... worth forgiving? What qualities do you see in me that make you want to even think about preserving this relationship?

If I turned out to be just like all the other girls you met. Then you deserve better, never settle. I am not worth you missing out on something better, something right.

If you trust the God in me enough to give me a second chance... than that also says a lot about how your relationship with Him is growing.

But if my mistake overshadows my worth... that means I wasn't who I presented myself to be in God. That means I'm a hypocrite.

But I was on your side of the grass once... And I know it hurts but I also know how much I'm dying for a second chance. Seriously, I'm emotionally dying inside.

None of the mistakes I made were worth not talking to you again. Nothing was worth losing your trust. You are worth much more than that. The tears I cried this Christmas day at the thought of how I may have hurt you or losing you... are all worth it.

But if I am not worth another chance, you are worth respecting. I will respect every decision that you make Chris. Even if it pains me. Even if it causes me to never want to settle for anything or anyone less than you. You ARE worth it."

From: Christopher Roberts

To: Karolyne Daudin

Date: Sun, Dec 25, 2011 at 7:04 pm

"I didn't make this decision lightly Kar trust me. And of course I've seen potential in u, and trust in u through God. But there's one thing that took me back.

U showed a sign of weakness when talking abt ur ex. U even admitted that its so hard not to see him, and just can't help urself from letting him in. N Everything I've been taking as a privelege is so easily given up.

This leads me to the real problem. Its not only the incident, its the fact that ur not even sure it won't happen again; and didn't give me any real reassurance that ur takin extra, or different steps to change this situation.

Wat do u think will be different? I'm not tryna walk into a trap. God told me to listen to u and truly hear ur full intentions.That's wat I wanna cover, the real issue, dispite any trust I have in u through God."

From: Karolyne Daudin

To: Christopher Roberts

Date: Sun, Dec 25, 2011 at 8:07 pm

"The real issue is that I haven't been applying what I learned from God. I didn't carry myself in a way that would make him take me seriously. The pictures I took with him and the way I would indulge in the time that we spent together are examples of how I transferred the wrong message to him.

For me to do better, the standards I set need to match the way I carry myself. My standard is that I don't want to have any close-knit or soul-tied relationship with him so I should carry myself in a way that presents distance and firmness.

I know that I want to get rid of this soul tie because I know it's unsafe. Accepting gifts and spending long amounts of time with him show that I wasn't applying this concept. I will do better by not just refusing to intentionally see him but keeping as much distance from his as possible.

If I need to cancel a photo shoot gig or delete him from social networking sites or avoid mutual friends... that's what I need to do. I need to be honest with my parents/family and let them know the deal. I need to be honest to all the people who we know in common.

Him and I have an understanding that God doesn't want us to be soul tied. If I let him ignore my wishes and we both don't accept God's word than I'm letting him sin and I need to hold him accountable too, when he tries to go against what God is saying.

I would settle for his disrespect towards my wishes.

Therefore, I wasn't standing firm in what I was saying.

I should've prayed for his understanding, respect, and relationship with God more. Prayer is powerful. I should've prayed for the strength to resist temptation. I should realize that sometimes forgiving goes with forgetting and I should've put God first. Most importantly, I should've remembered that without God, yes I am weak.

I sounded weak on the phone because for the longest time, I've been trying to fight this thing on my own strength. But for the first time yesterday, you fed me... spiritually. And you said "It's in God's hands". That's where I need to put and keep this situation and apply all that I've learned with his guidance and by his grace.

I already started making changes. I spoke to my mother about how I've made the decision to not talk to him anymore. He didn't have Christmas dinner here. I unfollowed him on twitter and he is no longer friends with me on facebook. I deleted his number and I'm going to sell the shoes that he got for me. I also prayed that God would give me the grace I needed to get through this.

Remember I told you about how my pastor was talking about when we are weak we are actually strong? Because God gives us His grace and that's His "translated power to us".

Yes I've taken similar steps in the past but my own strength wasn't enough to last very long. That's what's going to be the biggest difference this time around and it will make... a BIG difference."

From: Christopher Roberts

To: Karolyne Daudin

Date: Sun, Dec 25, 2011 at 10:46 pm

"I like the fact that you're applying what you've learned from God. And I hope that these steps help you to break this soul tie. I know that I'm not the reason you want this soul tie to be broken so I'm especially glad. Glad that you're doing it for yourself and for God. I'll like to talk to you tomorrow, its a lot to take in, and I wanna pray on it."

From: Christopher Roberts

To: Karolyne Daudin

Date: Sun, Dec 26, 2011 at 5:15 pm

"Well I had a lot to pray about and this is what I feel God was telling me. For our best interests we shouldn't continue our usual relationship. I'll be there to hear any breakthroughs you may have with applying the new changes you told me about yesterday. He told me that it is important that you and Him do this without any of my influences.

He's allowing us the opportunity to do things correctly. I prayed about it over and over and I kept getting the same answer. I didn't ask anything more because I trust that what He wants is for the best. I won't be contacting you just to be clear. But anything you feel you want to tell me, I'll be there to hear all you're going through and feeling. I feel like our trust in Him will bring us to a good place."

My Story: Out of Control

Now, where we went wrong is that less than a week later, on New Year's Eve, Chris and I made it official. Even though at the time it had seemed long overdue, something about it still didn't feel right. Maybe it was the fact that, only a few days before, we just communicated that we would not continue our usual relationship. Whatever it was, I didn't feel at ease, and of course now we know that it was wrong.

I mean, I did have a moment of hesitation. When he asked me to be his girlfriend, I did not jump and say "yes". Instead, I said, "I'll think about it." So I thought about it, and I prayed about it as well, and he said that he'd do the same. I felt the Holy Spirit leading me to take my time, and when I got back on the phone with Chris, he told me that the Lord told him to be patient with me. How did we miss that? We interpreted what the Spirit of the Lord had spoken inaccurately! Whether our interpretations were led by our own fleshly desires, I don't know. They probably were. We took what the Lord had spoken to us as a "go ahead" into our relationship as long as we took our time and didn't rush into intimacy. Now I realize that He was actually saying, "Be patient; take your time; do not rush into a relationship right now."

Minutes before the New Year of 2012, Chris and I were officially a couple. After winter break, I went back up to Tallahassee and things began rolling. Even though Chris was starting to get to know God and began growing in Him, we still were not on the same page and we were unequally yoked. I went in our relationship with the mindset of taking my time, but it wasn't very long until I started to compromise.

It all started the day after our talk in Chipotle, when I had compromised and kissed Chris. That moment set the tone for our relationship from that point on. Though we eventually did the bible study, started dating, went to church, I lost Chris's respect when I chose to compromise in that moment. He just wouldn't take me seriously after that!

Everything happened so fast. A lot of my standards were aborted while some remained intact. We began to kiss (I wish I would have saved it). I moved out of my apartment into a scholarship house, but the new chill spot was his crib, all the while still having bible study and going to church with him. I still kept the standard of no sex, no oral sex, etc., but I realized that the more we allowed ourselves to be in compromising situations, like being over at his house past 4:00 am, the more we were willing to disrespect the boundaries.

Still, some good came into play during that time. Chris reconnected with a cousin of his and had me come over one day to meet her. She was really cool, and I was happy to hear that she was a Christian, because I knew that she could be a good influence in his life. She and I became friends, and while Chris and I were dating, together her and I bought him his first bible.

Still, a month later, God intervened and commanded me to break up with Chris. At the time I didn't understand because, besides the lust issues, he was an awesome guy—yeah, there goes that compromising mindset again. Even though I enjoyed our relationship and there were so many practical qualities about him that I loved, but that does not excuse the fact that we were sinning.

I had to learn the hard way but at the end of the day all that matters is that I learned. I hope you that can learn from my mistakes and DO NOT COMPROMISE! God wants your whole heart! He wants more for you, and He wants the best for you. Set your standards and keep them. If the man or woman that you are talking to does not respect that, then tell them to bounce!

Of course it's easier said than done. Even though I finally let Chris go, I kept letting him back in because compromising had me flip-flopping in and out of obedience to God. After the first time that God told me to leave Chris alone, He probably had to tell me three or four more times before I actually let him go for real. The point where I let him go for real though was when Chris had actually begun to grow a fear for God and had been reading his bible. For the first time he was in agreement with what God was telling me. I can remember him saying, "I agree: if God says it, we need to obey." I was in shock. I even hesitated to let him go even then because those very words coming out of his mouth made him more attractive to me, but his obedience to God encouraged me to finally do the same.

That goes to show one of the major reasons why God says in His word, "Do not be yoked together with unbelievers. For what do righteousness and wickedness have in common? Or what fellowship can light have with darkness?" 2nd Corinthians 6:14 (New International Version). You may think that you can be a superhero and save the one that you are in a relationship with, but like the saying goes, "it's easier to pull someone off the chair than on the chair." You were not meant to be anyone's superhero. That is why Jesus came: to save. For the first time in my life, I was leaving it in His hands.

Towards the end of my spring semester, something happened. Something happened that would shatter my pride and bring my disobedience to a halt. Now that I look at it, it was one of the very best things that ever happened to me.

One of my friends from church, who had been attending Florida A&M University, the same university that Chris attended at the time, invited me to her college graduation, which took place at the end of April. I went and that morning I had a deep gut feeling that I was going to see Chris that day. Now that I look back on it, I see that it was a test. It was a warning from the Holy Spirit, who was preparing me for what would be coming forth in my day. Would I take the knowledge and insight that He had given me to obey Him?

Would I be faithful enough to go forth with avoiding and "casting down imaginations, and every high thing that exalteth itself against the knowledge of God" (2 Corinthians 10:5, King James Version)? Or would I use this knowledge to my own benefit to manipulate for what I wanted to come to pass?

After my girlfriend's graduation, in which the whole time I was antsy and anxious with the feeling of seeing Chris, I walked outside with my head down, looking at the pamphlet I had received during the ceremony to see if I'd find Chris's name on there. Then I heard a voice rise from Damaris, my bestie, from beside me, "Ohhh gosh" she said. I looked up, and right there in front of me was Chris in the flesh!

Between the last time, when we had agreed on being obedient and not speaking, and that moment, I had kept tabs on him from his cousin who had become my friend. That was probably wrong too. I learned that he was moving out of the place he lived with his friends to a community-living Christian home in Tallahassee. It was a home that fostered a culture of worship and righteous living and was void of major distractions like entertainment and media. Everyone who agreed to live in that home had to sign a contract of obedience that they would abide by the rules and restrictions of the house. His cousin lived there, and he had moved away from his old life of clubbing and selling daiquiris with his friends into this whole new environment that helped him grow exponentially in God. I had also learned from her that he had been offered different job opportunities out of state, and I was so proud of all he had been accomplishing.

When I saw him, we began talking and catching up. He asked me what I was doing at the graduation, and I told him why. Then I asked him if he was graduating, and he said that he would be later that evening. Automatically something went off in me that was like, "No, I have to be here; I can't miss his graduation. No, I need to go." That loud and anxious voice was pressed up against the faint whisper that told me to be obedient.

After he left I haphazardly drove off to the store where I bought him an assortment of graduation balloons, a card, and his favorite candy. I desperately wanted to be with him and support him in that season, but it was not my time to do so. I saved the little that I bought for his graduation in my car and went over to my friend's house for her barbeque celebration.

Bestie and I spent a good minute at the barbeque, but the time started approaching when I started telling my girlfriend and everyone there, "Ok guys, I have to go soon... I have another graduation to go to." Around the time where I would have to leave to make it early enough to find parking and get good seats at the graduation, Bestie and I left on our way. I was so prideful, so determined, so ready to be disobedient and share in this moment with him, meet his family, etc. Well guess what, I experienced another God intervention!

While driving up on one of Tallahassee's hills, my car began to slide back and it stopped in its tracks. It did not move and I never made it to Chris's graduation. I was immobile for a whole year! My car did not work from April 2012 to April 2013. In between that time I went back and forth between countless mechanics, but my car was more of a representation of what God was doing in me more than anything else. He was humbling me, showing me that I can trust Him, and that I must trust Him to take the reins and lead me. Here is a recent spoken-word poem that I wrote of the experience:

My Drive

"Smoke rose
like the nose
of a burning flame,
proud as can be
in the midst of the street
where everybody could see
it seep
from the hood
of my raggedy tragedy.
Forced out of the comfort
of my own car,
I came outside
to the side
and couldn't decide
if it was even worth it anymore.
With no more money to spend
and my patience running thin
I asked myself...
am I really going through this again?
Like every time I get it fixed
I find another glitch
who made this anyway?
It's imperfect in everyway.
I pray for a new car everyday.
I might as well give it away.
It's like a car note I can't pay.
Been at it for years—

if it isn't the gears
it's the transmission.
I was driving up a hill
like I was ready to conquer a mission
until I realized that it was mission
IMPOSSIBLE
when I began to slide back
beating the wind like dominoes
for another year my Ford never drove.
Instead,
it became a storage closet
for my good will clothes
I had the will to go
just no way to get there I suppose.
I wasn't dressed in a vehicle
that could transfer me
but my transformation you see
was birthed through God humbling me.
I had to take a whiff of the smoke
to realize that I was being choked
to hell as my destiny.
I had to STOP in front of everyone.
The girl on her grind and always on the run
came to realization that I let pride get the best of me.
Like the beats bouncing off me
and leaking loudly into the streets,
seeking the attention of the world when
I'm supposed to be set apart quietly
like the gentle and unfading beauty

from within me for others to see.
I was getting worked on
by the Mechanic
and couldn't stand it.
Wanted to go forward with my plans
and forgot the God
who created the stars and planets.
He spoke the world into existence
and didn't even have to plan it
but he still had a plan for me—
to prosper and not to harm me.
He knows every single part of me
from every plug to every port
from where I'm leaking and to my breaking point
so why would I point the finger at Him
when I'm the one not caring for my vehicle,
not presenting my body as a temple
or my life as an example?
I'm not pumping air in my tires
when I don't back up my words with actions.
I get into accidents when I don't pay attention.
My battery dies when I leave it on
like when I'm complacent and forget
to rev it up again.
My car stops on E
when I don't refuel
on what's keeping me—
keeping me from climbing up the haughty hill
when my mission exceeds my transmission

like God humbles us
 when our pride tries to compare us to Him.
I keep finding things wrong
like every sin reveals another sin
like stealing can turn into lying
and addiction into tradition
it all starts within.
My car was a reflection
of the life I chose to live in
and it was taken away
just like my breath can be
at any day.
I learned humility
and how to wait on others.
No longer had others waiting on me.
On the side of the street
I know what it feels like to be stung by a bee
cursing next to a tree, standing sturdy and tall
like I'm supposed to be
planted by the streams of water
yielding much fruit
and taking deep root in my source,
the Maker of heaven and earth, He is my reservoir.
I learned how it felt to thirst for Him
 standing in the hot sun
only to wait for the bus where I'd blend in.
No longer having control of where I was going
and leaving behind where I'd been
made me remember God again.

That He had always been my guide.
I was on the passenger's side
and told Him to pull to the side
so I could take this vessel for a ride
and chose my own direction.
Now I realize I'm rentin'
so I can be His reflection.
He gave me the keys
and told me to fully serve Him
so I'm no longer swerving'
but I'm going straight on the highway.
Knowing that I'll reach my final destination one day.
Picking up people along the way
and taking them with me.
Can't sleep on my destiny
because others' lives depend on me
and they're depending on you too.
So what are you gunna do?
There's a BMW out there waiting for you.
By the way
it stands for, By the Masters Way
Christ is the only way
let Him drive you, today."

"Know" Doesn't Mean "Now"

The summer after my freshman year in college, a lot of changes took place within me. God began doing a cleansing of all the dirt that I had piled up from my past relationships as well as all the insecurities, fears, and sins that I had accumulated.

I was in Brooklyn, New York, visiting my cousin and aunt around the time that things became deeply heated between my ex-fiancé and me. When the summer first began, I went back home, and though I did not go to his house or see him, we got back in touch by phone. While I was in New York, he and I had this big blow-up argument and he had reached his max with me.

We went back and forth on whether we would continue to try to work on our relationship, but at that point I was confused. I began to pray, "God, what do you want me to do? Who am I supposed to be with? I spent so many years with my ex, and I feel like You keep removing Chris from my life." I was just scared. Scared to death that I'd be alone for the rest of my life, and if I couldn't have Chris, I was willing to be comfortable and settle for my ex even despite his unfaithfulness.

It seemed like a dead-end road. My ex and I tried to work it out, but it was just a lost cause. He warned me, "Stay away from me; stay away from my family. Don't you dare come near me. I don't want anything to do with you again." He made it very clear, and the spirit of the Lord confirmed it for me. "Stay away from him."

I needed guidance. I needed to hear God clearly, so I did a day of fasting. I did an absolute fast where I had no water and no food for 24 hours. I spent the day in meditation and prayer, really trying to hear the voice of the Lord. I was taken to the book of Joshua.

In the book of Joshua, in the bible, starting in chapter three all the way to chapter seven, I studied and was inspired by the Holy Spirit on which steps to take next. The context in which the story takes place within the bible is that Joshua, Moses' previous aid who was now called by God to finish the leading of the Israelites into the promise land, leads them out of the wilderness to the crossing of the Jordan River, which is across from the Land of Jericho. After the Israelites cross the river into the land, they spend a few days near Jericho healing from a mass circumcision that took place. God was looking to consecrate them, those who had been born in the wilderness and had not yet been consecrated along the way. God wanted His people to be set apart, though the method of that today is only accomplished by pursuing righteousness through the salvation that can only come from Jesus Christ.

Shortly after celebrating the Passover, a tradition held by the children of Jerusalem to honor and commemorate the time in Egypt when the spirit of the Lord passed over the homes of the children of Jerusalem and wiped out the first-born sons of the Egyptians, the Israelites received direction from the Lord that that they should march around the walled-in city seven times with the priests blowing their trumpets, with the ark of the covenant following, and on the seventh day, after the loud blast from the priests on the trumpets, the people should have given a loud shout and cry so as to tear down the walls of Jericho. They did this, and the wall fell, and as commanded, they went in to ambush the town and burn everything in it, except to spare Rahab and her family, the women who had assisted and kept hidden two Israeli spies as well as retuning to the Lord the silver, gold, bronze, and iron for his treasury.

Yet one particular warning and command that the Lord had given was that no one go in and leave with any devoted thing from that city. As so it says in Joshua 6:18,

But keep away from the devoted things, so that you will not bring about your own destruction by taking any of them. Otherwise you will make the camp of Israel liable to destruction and bring trouble on it. (New International Version)

This was true. A man named Achan from the tribe of Judah coveted and took for himself a robe. Shortly thereafter, the Lord was angry and that which He had spoken came to pass: trouble came upon Israel, and when facing their enemy, from a region called Ai, thirteen men were killed. Joshua was extremely distraught and fell face down and began to question the Lord on why He would bring the Israelites all the way to the land to be destroyed by their enemies. It was then that the Lord revealed Israel's sin and disobedience towards Him because of the works of Achan. Then He commanded him,

"Go, consecrate the people. Tell them, 'Consecrate yourselves in preparation for tomorrow; for this is what the Lord, the God of Israel says: That which is devoted among you, O Israel. You cannot stand against your enemies until you remove it.'" Joshua 7:13 (New International Version).

As Joshua was bringing the tribes unto him, and at the presentation of Achan, the man confessed what he did, and he and his family were stoned and all of his possessions were burned for what he had done. It was then the Israelites were able to go and overcome their enemy, Ai.

During my bible study, there were significant things that stood out to me as the Holy Spirit led. I began receiving confirmation on what to do as far as my situation was concerned. To me, Jericho was a walled-up city, filled with devoted things that needed to be burned... like the soul tie that I had to my ex. I was also like Israel: God was calling me to be consecrated, separate for Him. He was calling me to be obedient. He was calling me to break down the walls with my worship and praise. He was calling me to take all my treasures and valued things from within me and give them to Him, to His very own treasury. God simply wanted my heart. From this revelation He gave me further instruction, and my deliverance began.

He showed me ways in which I could take this experience and apply it to my life and my situation. I had to get rid of everything in my life that devoted me to, or even tied me to, my ex. That meant I had to cut off all connection from mutual friends, from his family members, etc. Every picture on my phone and on my computer, every love letter and every message, every little thing... I had to let it go. Yet at that moment, I only dealt with letting go of those physical things outside of me. Later on I'd realize that the soul tie didn't have as much to do with my possessions, as it had to do with my heart.

Weeks earlier, I had made a commitment to God that I would not date for three years. My heart was torn, and I knew that I had spent a majority of my teen years in and out of relationships. I hadn't had the chance to experience what it really meant to have a relationship with Jesus without cheating on Him with everything else in this world. During that time in New York, my desire for consecration and the depths of the vow that I made to Him grew deeper within me. I really wanted to obey God and trust Him, and I began to feel him tugging at my heart. He was bringing me out of the shadow of my sin, to a place where I was walking on Holy Ground.

Ground Level

So many saved souls
are stuck
on ground level.
Because just like gravity,
there's and invisible force
called Adam's seed
that causes their souls,
their feet,
to meet,
the floor,
everytime.
They step forward;
heading for a place
that will never be reached
unless they lift up their heads
and whole-heartedly beseech
to rise with the Son rise
Jesus Christ.
But their eyes still lie on the horizon
even after the Son has risen.
Their horizontal perspectives
and artificial visions
causes them to neglect the very essence
of the eternal life that they've been given.
And even though they were forgiven
in their sin
God didn't mean for them

to continually give in
to sin
but to have a new heart
and a new spirit within.
God wants them to elevate in Him
but they gravitate to the same ground
where their old life begins;
still bound
to their shadow of sin.
And as long as they forsake
their potential latitudes
that shadow will ALWAYS be there
leaving them to cling to old attitudes.
So I beg of you,
stop looking ahead
but raise your head,
If you are still on the ground
that God didn't call you to tread.
Don't go that way
because Jesus Christ is the only way
and the bible does say that,
"He brought me out of the slimy pit
and out of the miry clay
He set my feet upon a rock
and He established my way".
But so many people get saved
and still pave
their own pathways
expectin' to drive through

like salvations' a drive through
but you cant
have it your way
because it's not Burger King
and you're not being served by man
you got served by the
King of Kings
and he paid the price for
EVERYTHING
so you don't have to add
anything
to His sacrifice
no condiments or combinations
because
JESUS CHRIST
is the
full compensation
and complete course
for our
salvaton
and I say that
without a doubt.
BUT don't be a one-night stand
stay around
and work it out.
because we're still slaves to sin
when we don't fully let God in.
We leave Him on the porch
and He becomes our last resort

unless were really in need...
then we'll take what He's supplying
and if were really in some trouble
then we're ready for
relying.
A lot of us got saved
because we had a fear of dying
but our mindset needs to change
Because not even death
could keep Christ chained.
So please don't leave
the way you came.
Too many
new lives
hardly
last.
But after a few re-dedications
some of us finally got it right.
Something started to change
in the direction of our sight.
Something about our perceptions
had found a new light.
We drew closer to the Son.
Our souls began to take flight.
Our hearts began to thirst for God,
with new minds that chase understanding
Wanting to give to Him,
what He's deservingly demanding.
Keeping his decrees

and never compromising
what His Word's commanding.
And the only way
we left
that old place
where we were standing
was because God so loved the world,
That He gave
His one and only
begotten son
Jesus Christ
that who so ever believes in him
would not perish,
but have Everlasting Life!
And the only way we
stopped going back
to that old place
where we were standing
was because God
chose
to give us
a new heart
towards Him.
"He said
I'll give you a new heart
and new spirit within."
So no longer do you have to live,
in the shadow of your sin.
Your new seal is His Spirit

until the day we all ascend, with Him.

Little did I know I would go through the process of deliverance until I was whole. Like in Philippians 1:6 (New International Version) where it says, "being confident of this, that he who began a good work in you will carry it on to completion until the day of Jesus Christ." Even before the completion, you could see God working in my life to bring his promises to pass. There was no such thing as Him waiting to do it because God is an eternal being and not locked into the confines of time. When He speaks, at that very moment His word is life and flesh. Because God began a good work in me, there is no doubt that I was already fully delivered, even when I could not see it with my natural eyes. By faith I believed it, and now I am able to see and share the fruit of my deliverance in the world.

Before seeing it, I still qualified for the promises that came with my deliverance. As soon as you are IN Christ and OUT of sin, all things that belong to the Father are made available to you. Like John 15:7 (New International Version) says, "If you remain in me, and my words remain in you, ask whatever you wish, and it will be done for you."

In the past, when I asked the Lord for a husband, I wasn't abiding in Him; rather, I was into myself. Deliverance is a process of escape that moves you away from those things that separate you from God, which in turn, brings you closer to Him. "No temptation has overtaken you except what is common to mankind. And God is faithful; He will not let you be tempted beyond what you can bear. But when you are tempted, He will also provide you with a way out so that you can endure it" 1 Cor. 10:13 (New International Version).

Now during my deliverance process, I saw the Lord speaking to me in many different ways and reassuring me of His promises to me, with one of them specifically being the promise of me having a husband one day.

I was walking down the streets of downtown Manhattan one day after leaving brunch with my cousin and aunt. As I lifted my head higher to view the cityscape, before me on a billboard in big letters was the word "DREAM." At that moment, I automatically felt like there was something about that sign. I was very close to telling my cousin, but I decided to keep it to myself because I was not sure of what it was.

A few days later, my cousin, aunt, uncle, and I took a road trip up to Montréal, Canada, to see my other aunt and cousin. When we got there, my aunt presented us with gifts, and a special part of our gifts was perfumes. She explained how she tried to give us perfumes with names she thought suited us. My perfume was called "DREAM." I was a little taken aback by this second occurrence of the word. I began to wonder if it was just a weird coincidence.

I made it back to my home in South Florida a few days later, and my cousin had decided to go with me. One day while we were sitting in my room, talking about our families and so on, we stumbled upon the topic of my sister's name, Lola. That's what everyone in the family calls her. We talked about its origin from the song, "Whatever Lola wants, Lola gets," but

Lola is only her middle name. Her real name, which is the name that her teachers and friends call her at school, is not often used among us. Come to find out, my cousin never even knew what her real name was. So when I told her she asked me, "What does it stand for?" and I looked it up right then and there, and come to find out, it stood for "DREAM."

That was the third time, and I couldn't hold it in, but before I could even say anything, my cousin was like, "Hey, didn't Tati give you a perfume that said, 'Dream'?" She was way ahead of me! She didn't even know about the billboard that I had initially seen. I ended up telling her that I thought God was trying to tell me something, and I told her about the billboard, and from then on we both went into a secret mini investigation, trying to figure out what God was trying to show me.

One of her hypotheses was that God was telling me that I don't dream enough and that a lot of the different issues going on in my family could actually make a big turnaround and change. For some reason, though, that hypothesis did not resonate with me. Of course I believed there could be a big change in my family... God did not have to tell me to dream for that. I could not put my finger exactly on what it was that God was trying to show me, but I knew it wasn't that I don't dream enough. I am the biggest dreamer I know, more specifically, a woman of Faith. I believe that God can do absolutely anything. That's probably why I paid attention to the "dream" occurrences anyway in the first place. Because I am very alert to my surroundings and I am always waiting in hope and anticipation of what God is going to do next. Some would call it "the posture of expectancy."

In the midst of all this, my process of deliverance was continuing. I felt moved by a suggestion given by my aunt from Canada. She told us of an exercise she did where she wrote down all of her sins and everything from her past on a piece of paper, then prayed over it, burned it, and gave it to God. She said that after she burned it, the words "no more crumbs, Jesus Satisfies" was left, and she really felt deliverance from that experience. What inspired my aunt to get rid of the "crumbs" was a sermon from T.D Jakes. My cousin and I agreed that we would one day try the exercise ourselves. So we did.

Let me tell you, by the end of writing everything down, my hand was sore. I had pages on top of pages on top of pages. She requested that when we do it we not only be one hundred percent honest, but we go into as much detail as possible. I had names on there. I had dates and times. I even listed specific acts of sexual immorality that I had committed and with whom I committed them. I just needed to be real with God. I listed all my exes, even Chris. I asked the Lord for forgiveness for putting my relationships and men before Him for so long. I asked Him to heal me and change my nasty heart. Yet most distinctly, I prayed for freedom. I asked the Lord to just break the chains and set me free from everything that was holding me back from being made whole. To break the chains from everything that was holding me back from giving myself fully to Him. Then as I burned the paper, I felt an overwhelming weight being lifted off of me. It's not really something that I could even describe.

The funny thing is, one word out of everything I wrote wouldn't burn. I promise, I spent fifteen extra minutes trying to burn that last little piece of paper, but eventually I just gave up and accepted that this is something that refused to go down in the flames. That word was "free." To this day, I still have that little piece of paper and keep it somewhere safe to remember. That was definitely one of the most amazing moments of my life.

The day after that I was on the patio of my Floridian home, just spending sweet time in the Lord's presence, when I heard the Holy Spirit whisper, "You're going to see Chris when you get back to Tallahassee." I jumped up in my chair. I was like, "I rebuke that, I cast down vain imaginations in Jesus name." At the time of course I thought it was the enemy who was trying to get me to be disobedient. Then I heard the Lord assuring me that it wasn't, but part of me did not want it to be true. I did not want to see Chris. Not after all this deliverance, writing down his name, burning it, and not to mention my three-year vow of singleness to God! I could not believe it. I told myself, "I don't know if this is the enemy or the Holy Spirit, but I will not make a move, and I won't believe it until I see it."

That weekend my family and I took a road trip to Orlando, Florida, for vacation. We were going to meet with other family from Atlanta, Georgia, and stay together in a nice resort suite. During the drive up, we got into conversation about different things we wanted to accomplish in life, and I realized that I had never asked my mom what she felt like her purpose was, or what it was that she had always wanted to do. The first thing that she opened her mouth and said was, "We all have a dream." Immediately I turned my head back to face my cousin, and we made eye contact like, "It's happened again!"

When we got to the hotel, I began unpacking the things in my bag. I found a perfume that I had thrown in my bag after rummaging and finding it in my grandma's drawer, who had borrowed it from me long ago. At that moment of packing I had not really looked at it, but while unpacking, I pulled it out, and right there on the bottle it said "DREAM." I was thinking, "How many people make perfumes called 'Dream'?" It wasn't even the same brand as the one my aunt gave me. That was the fifth time that the word "dream" had come up, and by that time I was rigorously praying to God. "Daddy, what are you trying to show me? What am I doing wrong? What's going on?" No answer.

Then the next day we all got up and got ready to go to Disney World, The Magic Kingdom, "Where Dreams Come True." The whole day in that park I was showered with "dream, dream, and dream." The song from the parade went, "A dream is a wish your heart makes when you're fast asleep," and so on. I was getting a little frustrated like, "What is it, God? What is it?"

Then that night I went to sleep, and I had a dream. In my dream, I walked into this apartment and I saw Chris sitting at this long dining table; he was doing something on a laptop. It's funny, because in the dream I felt like I was watching the dream but detached from it, not actually a part of it, even though I saw myself in it. It felt more of like a vision. I saw Chris sitting at the table, and I remember thinking to myself, "What is Chris doing here?" I was dressed in a navy blue professional business suit and heels, and I had something that looked like a briefcase in my hand. I don't even dress like that now. I walked in and stood in this apartment filled with pictures of Chris and I that I had never seen before. I remember one picture with Chris and me with my little brother and sister from the dream so distinctly; we were like on the sidewalk of an outdoor mall or outlet. I was thinking, "When did we take all these pictures?" Then, while I was standing at the door, he got up from the table, where he was doing something on a laptop, and came over all happy and said, "Hi baby," and landed me a pop kiss on the lips. I was thinking, "Oh my goodness, he did not just do that; we're not allowed to kiss. What's going on here!" Then he walked into the kitchen, where I followed him, and I saw my mom there cooking. He began speaking to her in Creole, and I was thinking, "Who taught Chris how to speak Creole?" My mom is Haitian, and I speak Haitian Creole fluently. Then he grabbed something from above the microwave and handed it to me and said, "Here's your salad, baby." I was thinking, "Salad? Why do I get salad if my mom's cooking food?"

Then I woke up and just lay there. After a few seconds I was like, "Wait, I just had a dream," and I began to remember my dream, and immediately I asked God, "Woah! What was that about?" I am used to getting dreams from Him, but never like that. The Holy Spirit then revealed to me that was my seventh encounter with a "dream" in the past three weeks and Chris was going to be my husband one day.

Yet just because you know he or she is the one, that does not necessarily mean that now is the time you should be with that person. The type of "know" that I am talking about is the type where God has revealed it to you, or you have gotten confirmation that this person is supposed to be your husband or wife.

The reason I say this "type of 'know'" is because people usually do not get to know who their spouse is through some prophetic dream or word from God, and nothing is wrong with that. For many, they simply go through the season of courting, which is the interview process of getting to know a potential mate that you consider spending the rest of your life with and then later on make the decision of whether or not you really know you want to be with that person.

Really knowing for yourself is very important, because even if you know straight from God what He has promised you, you don't want to miss the development that comes with the crucial season of courting and engagement. This is the mistake that I made. I knew who my husband was from God, so I neglected the opportunity to take the time to truly get to know him as a person.

I understand now why the Lord told me that I would be seeing Chris again. I was eventually going to marry him, even though I still didn't want to believe he would be back in my life so early. I was so adamant about keeping my three-year vow of singleness that I made to God after he took Chris out of my life. I planned on staying focused on Him alone. I was so excited about falling in love with Him and Him being the only love in my life at the time.

Yet there was absolutely nothing that I could do to keep what God had spoken from coming to pass. I spent the rest of the summer trying to convince myself that I had voices in my head and that I would never see Chris again. Yet another part of me knew that I had no control over what God was doing, even if I talked myself out of believing it. I believed that Chris was going to be my husband; I just didn't want him to come back into my life so early. I was so set on serving God with no distractions.

Soon enough though, the Lord was leading me to pray and fast for Chris heavily as well as for myself because I started getting drawn away by my own lusts. Towards the end of the summer, I spent a few weeks in Jamaica and had issues controlling my thoughts that grew very impure and lustful towards Chris.

I really needed the Lord's help on how to control my mind when it started thinking about the future because I would think about the wedding, then the honeymoon, and the rest was history. Over time, God helped me redirect my thoughts towards Him. I went to scripture for my ammo against the enemy. "Finally, brothers and sisters, whatever is true, whatever is noble, whatever is right, whatever is pure, whatever is lovely, whatever is admirable—if anything is excellent or praiseworthy—think about such things" Phil. 4:8 (New International Version).

I thought about Chris a lot during that time. I would picture in my head how everything would happen. If I were to see him again, we would be friends for two and a half more years, and then get married, and by that time I would have finished college. That was my plan. I would spend those years writing him love letters about how I knew the big secret of him being my husband before he even asked me to marry him and give him all the letters in origami hearts as a wedding present. I only ended up writing one letter.

Around the time that the new semester was approaching, I began looking for a ride back up to Tallahassee for school. His cousin said she could take me. We had planned to leave South Florida early in the morning because of the eight-to-nine-hour drive, but many things started to come up. Already I could see God working, and by the circumstances I could tell how everything would play out.

Because things kept coming up with her family and so on, we ended up leaving later than planned. Also, it was raining heavily most of the time, so for much of the ride we had to drive slower than the speed limit. It seemed like we would be getting back to Tallahassee late, so I called my house manager for the scholarship house that I lived in to see if I'd be able to check in later. It turned out that she would not be home, so I wouldn't be able to, and when I called my roommate, she also had plans for the night and would not be home to let me in. When I expressed the final verdict to Chris's cousin, that I wouldn't be able to return home that night, she offered that I stay at her place, and then she would just drop me home the next morning.

I spent the night there. I kept telling myself and the Holy Spirit the whole night, "I'm not gunna see him, I'm not gunna see him. I'm about to go to sleep. Alicia and I will wake up in the morning, and she'll take me straight home. I'm not gunna see him." Yet something kept telling me that I was going to see him before I left in the morning. I was just so nervous! I did not feel ready to see the man who I knew I would be spending the rest of my life with!

The next morning I woke up and went into the bathroom to get ready to leave. Then when I finished getting ready, I walked out and turned to walk down the hall, and there he was! He reacted in delightful shock, and the words, "Kar? What are you doing here?" slowly slipped out of his mouth. I reacted, sighing with a smile on my face, "Hi Chris," and I explained to him why I was there. Then he lead me to the couch, and we began to catch each other up on what we had missed the passed few months.

I was blown away and so pleased to hear everything that he had to say. He just seemed so excited about his new relationship with God. He got saved, got baptized, was speaking in tongues, was spending daily time with the Lord, and shared with me a few revelations he had written down in his new worship journal. It was amazing! He also went on to tell me about his decision to remain abstinent because he did not want to sin against his future wife or against God. It's amazing what God can do in a matter of months that we can't do in a million years. I couldn't save Chris. It was only up to me to leave him alone with the Lord. Now he is forever changed.

We had been catching up while I was waiting for his cousin to get ready to take me home. I felt the Holy Spirit say that Chris was going to take me home and help me move in. Then I began to tell myself, "No he's not, his cousin is taking me home, and this will be the last time I'm seeing Chris." Then she walked into the living room, all anxious and frenzied, and said, "I don't think I can take you home. I'm running late, and I have to get a lot of things together for the wedding. I need to go straight there. Can Chris take you home?" Then he automatically accepted the task, and I was thinking, "Ok, God."

So we ended up taking all of my stuff out of her car and transferring it to his. Then he took me home and helped me move in. Before he left, we talked a little more and decided it would be cool if we exchanged numbers and just be there for each other as friends, to support each other.

From then on we started hanging out. Chris had gotten several visions about me relating to me being his wife and just had a deep feeling that I was. A few weeks into us hanging out, we started playing this game that he began that went something like this: "I know," "You know what?" "I know what you don't know," "No, I know what you think you know that I don't know," and so on.

Then one day we went out to eat and we got into the "I know" game. I was just hoping the "I know" game would last for the next two and a half years and we would leave it at that, because I was still on my three-year vow of singleness to God and I was not looking to break it. Then Chris said, "Do you really know?" I said, "Yes, I know." Then he said, "How do you know? Did you see a wedding dress?" Then I gave him this piercing look like, "What the heck, bro? You just messed up the game," then I turned my head to the side, and I looked down and sighed. I began saying, "This is awkward, awkwerdddd, AWKWARD." It was blank, quiet, for a good minute. Then I began to tell him the story about how I knew, and he began to share his visions with me as well.

We got into a conversation about how crazy it is that we knew, but also how cool it was. We were talking about purpose. There must be a reason that God would reveal it to us both at this time. We discussed how we must have a special assignment and a duty to stay focused. We both didn't think we'd be getting married anytime soon because Chris acknowledged my vow and purity ring.

We began to hang out a lot more, and people began to question. "Is he your boyfriend?" "Are you guys talking?" etc. Many people made weird comments like, "He looks like the hubby type," or "I can see y'all getting married," and I'd be like, "Well I don't know. We'll see about that." It was a huge secret. The only people who knew were God, Chris, and me, along with his cousin and my best friend, who I eventually told. I felt peace to tell her towards the end of the summer.

Then soon enough I became torn. I became torn with the fact that I was so determined to do this three-year singleness thing and Chris, my future husband, was right there in my face. Not only that, for as much as I hung around him and still claimed that I was single and nothing was going on, our relationship began looking ungodly to everyone, and it began to seem like I was hiding something bad.

My best friend Damaris eventually brought this issue to my attention. "You and Chris might as well court. It looks to everyone that that's what you guys are doing anyway." "But Bestie! I made a three-year vow to God that I would not date." "That's honorable," she said. "But you made the three-year vow. God did not tell you to, and it just may not be His will for you to be single for three years. You have to pray and go to Him about that. I am sure that He sees your heart and loves that you would even commit to making a vow like that to Him, but regardless, He just may have other plans for you, so just make sure that you are sure about doing this three-year thing."

Finally, I went to God about it. I had been ignoring Him and fighting Him on this thing the whole time. I did not want to hear what He had to say because I knew what it was. He brought Chris back into my life for a reason. That reason in that season simply was to court him and get to know him. Unfortunately, that reason was not that obvious to me at the time. We made the mistake of speeding up the whole courting part and going straight into engagement!

Now, nine months into our engagement, while I'm writing this book, is now when I realized, before saying yes to the ring, I never got to know him for myself. I did not put in the time to interview him in order to confirm in my own heart that he was the one I wanted to spend the rest of my life with. We spent the past five months trying to get this wedding thing to come to pass, and it never did, and now I see why. The manipulation I did in the beginning of our relationship, in trying to be in Chris's life out of season was now biting me in the butt. Trust me, knowing who your future husband is and still not being able to marry him because God is taking you back to complete the steps you missed is not fun. I can almost bet that if I did it God's way from the beginning, Chris and I would have been married by now. Sometimes trying to control things and doing it your own way actually prolongs the situation. Especially if God wants the best for you and He loves you enough to keep intervening until you get it right.

Though he is destined to be my husband, there are still things that need to be done. I can't just jump from point A to point Z. God did not reveal to me who my husband was so that I can hurry up and rush into marriage. God revealed to me who my husband was so that I can prepare and equip myself to be with the man that I was specifically designed for. God revealed to me who Chris was so that I can pray for him by name, prepare to cater to his spiritual needs and growth so that we can get to the place where we are both ready. Chris is a newly saved Christian; it's only been a year. Yes, he has grown tremendously! Yet there is still more growing that needs to be done not only in him but also in me before we get married. God has brought him back into my life, not to fulfill my own selfish desires but simply to be there for him as we grow in the seasons before we get married.

Part Two

The Preparation of Singleness

When I dated, my downward spiral of disobedience lasted longer than it should have. I was focused on finding a man who could make me feel loved and affirmed instead of taking the time to develop a relationship with God. I had a deep fear of singleness. The word "singleness" to me meant loneliness, weakness, and shame. Of course, now I know that that was a lie from the pits of hell.

Today is a new day, because I eventually made the decision to give my heart fully to God when I made that three-year vow. Even though it only lasted nine months, the value and preciousness that was birthed out of that time were worth it. Singleness is a special season. It is actually a blessing from God.

When I was single, I got to spend long hours basking in the Lord's presence. I still get to spend time with Him, but not in the same way, because part of my focus has shifted to doing what I need to do in the world in order to prepare for marriage. Then, when I am married, I will have a lot of responsibilities and priorities added to the list; I know it won't be the same.

When you are single you are able to do things like go on missions and serve God fully in whatever way you desire without having to ask or answer to anyone, except your parents of course if you're still a child. Even now, being engaged, I can't just jump up and take a three-month mission trip without talking to Chris about it. I can't just do anything I want however I want. I'm in a relationship now, and I have to have the courtesy of respecting and communicating to my fiancé.

Singleness is a season of preparation, not preparation just for marriage, but for courting, and engagement as well. Sometimes we may have the tendency to skip over those stages and ask ourselves, "Am I ready to get married?" when we are only in the stage of singleness. When you actually think about it, engagement is actually where you become fully prepared for marriage because God takes you through the process. For the singles, I would recommend that you first look into whether or not you are prepared to court someone before deciding whether or not you are ready to marry someone.

Pressing Questions:

Have I really taken the time out to get to know Jesus, with no distractions, no idols, and no ill intentions?

What have I learned during my season of singleness?

Was my season of singleness cut short by a distraction, and is God calling me back to lie at His feet?

Dealing With & Letting Go of The Past

During my season of singleness, one of the biggest things that God dealt with me on was my past. You saw how much damage that my past caused to my relationship with Chris when we first started talking. Still having ties to my ex opened up doors for the enemy to move, and it resulted not only in me hurting Chris, but in sin as well. For a long time throughout our relationship, Chris did not trust me and always thought that I was up to something.

It was not until recently that I finally gained his trust back. Before then, he would express to me that my relations with my ex gave him a reason not to trust me and that it would take time for me to gain it back.

Decisions I made in the past had a major effect on my present relationship and almost broke us up. When I was single, God made it clear that I should cut all ties with my exes. Not only that, but he revealed and removed fake friends and people out of my life and dealt with me on the issues of lust that I had.

Do not question God on why he hasn't brought you your husband or wife if you know that there are still a lot of things hidden in your closet. Don't you know those bones will have to come out sooner or later? I mean you are not going to be perfect when you meet that special person, but thank God that you will be renewed! You will be whole. You won't be looking for someone else to make you whole. If not, the enemy will just use that hole in your heart to enter into your relationship and break you down.

Repentance is important. It brings deliverance. Remember, God revealed my husband to me a little after I wrote down all the sins of my past in detail, asked for repentance, and put it in His hands. I told Him to set me free. I'm not saying to do that just so God will reveal to you your husband, but a repentant heart is one that God will definitely work with.

Pressing Questions:

What has God already delivered me from? How do I think that can help me bring Him glory in my current/future relationship?

What things or people am I still holding on to from my past? How are those things influencing my relationship with God and the relationships with those around me? Is it negative?

Have I taken the time to repent and turn from the wrong that I've done? Have I gotten to the point of begging God for a new clean heart?

Karolyne Roberts

Spirituality

When you are single, God will be working on your heart, your heart towards Him. Don't get me wrong: you have a part to play in this too. You have to look deep down inside and see what's in there. Are there things in there that are not like Him? What is ruling you? What is moving you? Are you moved by your love for Christ? Or are you moved by attention from men? Have you surrendered all to Him? Are you manipulative? Have you made Him a priority? Or do you only go to Him for what you want? Do you only pray to Him when you're praying about your husband, or do you pray for others as well? Do you really have a relationship with Christ? Wondering and asking how His day is going?

You can come to know Jesus and have a relationship with Him at ANY point in your life. Even on your deathbed, He can accept you. I've got to say though, using the season of singleness to know Jesus is unique. You will be comforted in that season to know that He is your husband—your everything. What is He specifically for you, though? Because of my life and what I've been through in my relationship with God, I identify with Him specifically as my Daddy, and that's the unique bond we share. You may identify with Him specifically as your Healer, your Comforter, or your Best Friend. Though He is everything, realizing who He has been for you specifically in your life will draw you closer to Him spiritually, and He will draw closer to you in return. My whole unique relationship with God is centered on me seeing Him and interacting with Him as my Daddy.

Use your season of singleness to begin pouring out to God. Stop gossiping to your friends and express to Him where it hurts. When you hurt, He hurts with you. He can look into the deepest core of you and understand. He is your Creator.

Pray to Him, not religiously, but relationally. He wants to hear from you. Practice characteristics like faithfulness and submission by first being faithful and obedient to God. Get involved in church, not for the looks, but because of your dedication to Him. Join a ministry. Seek out what it is that he wants you to do with your life. Discover your purpose. All of this will be done in preparation to not only beginning a relationship with a potential life partner, but also setting the foundation of your relationship with Christ for eternity. The purpose is way bigger and extends outside of you wanting someone to cuddle you at night. This will prepare you for courting. In courting you have a lot of questions to ask. If you skip out on setting a strong foundation in your season of singleness, you won't experience what you need to in order to ask the right questions and value the right answers.

Pressing Questions:

Do I understand the purpose? My purpose, God's purpose, and the purpose of courting and marriage?

Have I gotten involved with the things of God? Or am I running to God with my own agenda?

Who is God, specifically, to me?

Patience and Waiting Level One

Patience and waiting in singleness is level one. If you were rushing to get to the next step so that you can stop waiting, I have got some news for you! Sorry to burst your bubble, but the waiting is even rougher when you get to the next stage. The closer you get, the more you anticipate, and the harder it becomes to wait. Ask the Holy Spirit constantly to develop His fruits within you so that you can bear the fruit of patience. I have to do it everyday.

During singleness, God will develop patience in you, because, trust me, you will need to apply those skills of waiting during engagement, especially if you are looking to honor God in your courtship and engagement by remaining pure until marriage. Even though I am a virgin, this was especially hard for me in the beginning because I've been waiting all my life and I'd like to get to it. Yes I said that. By the grace of God though, and only by His grace, I kept the cookies in the cookie jar.

Expect to prepare during singleness by waiting. God is developing your span of patience. Maybe write a book like me while you're waiting. Start a business, pick up a new hobby, do something! Trust me, there are tons of things that you can find to do; just don't let purposeful distractions end up distracting you from your purpose. "But let patience have her perfect work, that you may be perfect and entire, lacking in nothing." (James 1:4, King James 2000 Bible)

Waiting has been a challenge for me, especially in this season of my engagement. Chris and I decided that we couldn't just kiss, have sex, or do whatever our flesh felt at any moment. If we were going to honor God, we had to do so intentionally and with all our hearts. We verbally spoke about this and agreed upon it. We are not going to have sex or kiss until marriage.

Now Chris and I have spent a lot of time together, a lot of private time too. I would not recommend that, but by the grace of God we have been able to make it this far and still remain pure, though unfortunately, we encountered moments heated temptation along the way. It's so hard to spend so much time with the man that I know is going to be my husband while still having the patience to wait for that day when it's official in the eyes of God and in the eyes of government, not just in our eyes. If our eyes and our minds were the justifier of what we do, then we could do anything we wanted. Please do not use excuses like, "But I already feel like he's my husband, so it's ok," or, "We are married in our hearts."

The thing you have got to remember and always remind yourself is, until it is official, you haven't earned the right to have them physically. It is not until marriage that the body of another person should belong to you sexually, and the bible makes it clear. 1 Corinthians 7:4 (New International Version), "The wife does not have authority over her own body but yields it to her husband. In the same way, the husband does not have authority over his own body but yields it to his wife." Yet in the meantime, the Holy Spirit should be the one living within us and we should offer up our bodies as living sacrifices unto God as long as we are on this earth.

Furthermore, when you realize that the Holy Spirit is living within you, you will not only have the knowledge to know how you should be living and honoring God with your body, but you will also know the strength and power vested within you to wait.

Pressing Questions:

Have I been bearing the fruits of the spirit talked about in Galatians 5:22–23?

What do I spend most of my time doing? What do I spend most of my time thinking about?

Do I show signs of anxiety and rashness? Do I lack self-control?

The Importance of Courting

Courting is so very important! It is the basis of you making the decision of whether or not you would like to spend the rest of your life with someone. Courting creates the foundation of the confidence in yourself and between you and your spouse that you guys are the best persons in the entire world for one another. It is the building up and the building towards laying a solid foundation for marriage.

You won't know who "the one" is as long as you're in sin. I am not talking about slipping here and there. None of us are perfect. I am talking about it habitual sin. I am talking about making deliberate decisions, sometimes even planning ahead of time, to indulge in sin. That's what it means to be living in sin and not actively pursuing righteousness.

Before even worrying about meeting the one or who the one will be, we need to repent. We need to repent of all our sins and iniquities, have a true change of heart, mind, and life.

God has given man free will. So therefore, you have the opportunity to get to know someone and make them your choice or not. If your are in Christ and being led by the Holy Spirit, your choice will inevitably be God's choice for you as well. So while you're living for the Lord, if you have chosen to make someone "the one" after they have courted you and are on the same page with you spiritually, then the question is not "is this person the one?"

The question is, "Am I willing to commit to this person, for the rest of my life?" Commitment is a decision you make, not a result of fate. It takes work to love someone unconditionally and to decide that you will stick it out with them for richer or for poorer, in sickness and in health, till death do you part.

Openness

When it comes to considering whether or not you want to spend the rest of your life with someone, you need to be ready to be transparent, open, and honest. This is not a decision to mess with or take lightly. You need to be willing to share and willing to ask. You want to prepare for "until death do us part" and not "until divorce do us part." Many times divorce happens because there is a lack of communication and openness before the marriage takes place. Then, in the marriage, the couple begins to struggle with the miscommunication, when marriage has all its other parts that need to be dealt with.

You need to be open and honest about your past! Tell your spouse everything! Tell them where you grew up, how you grew up, who was there, who wasn't there, what you used to do, what you stopped doing, what you continued to do, why you started, why you stopped, why you continued, etc. These are just examples of things you should be open enough to share so that your spouse can get a better understanding of where you came from and be able to prepare themselves to handle and understand things better if and when they come up later on. If you keep information from the one you are looking to marry, you are just leaving another open door for the enemy to come in.

Consider this: not only will your honesty and openness bring you and your spouse closer to one another, you just may find out that you have something in common with your spouse from the past, that you both can empathize with each other about and help each other grow past. Or you may find out that you have two different areas that complement each other, and then you can help each other with those areas.

When Chris and I both opened up and shared our past, we both had in common an addiction to pornography. Since we have both been delivered, we use this commonality from our past to be on the same accord concerning purity in our present. The reason we can be on the same page and share the same goal concerning purity is because we both know that we suffered from the same weakness.

One thing that Chris and I found different about our pasts was how we were raised. He grew up in an orderly household with mom, dad, and all his siblings in the same house. I grew up in a single-mother household with two half sisters, and my dad was married to another woman and lived with my two other half siblings. I always felt parts of me missing and really struggled because of that. Family is very important to Chris, and I am happy that God has blessed me with a family man that can help me walk against the past troubles in my own life and make a better life for my children.

Talk about the future! Ask questions about one another's visions. See if you share the same gifts and whether or not God has given you similar and compatible revelations about life and about what he wants you to do. How do you feel about kids? How do you want to live, and what kind of lifestyle do you want to have? If you and your partner have two completely different agendas, it is definitely something to pray about and consider. You don't want to start a union divided. Remember, open doors give room to the enemy!

Get to know as much as you can about the one that you are courting! No question is too big or too small. Granted, you won't find out everything, but you want to know as much as possible before making that big step. Still, you guys will continue to grow and learn through engagement, and even throughout marriage.

Knowing For Yourself

Knowing for yourself that this is the person you want to be with is important. That's the part that Chris and I missed when we went into engagement. We knew because God revealed it to us, but we didn't know because we hadn't really taken the time to study one another. We made the decision in our heads that "this is the one I am meant to be with," but we skipped the part of making the decision in our hearts that "this is the one I want to be with." We completed that step during engagement, when it should have actually been done before engagement, before saying yes to the ring.

Engagement is a promise to be married. We were still trying to know for ourselves in the midst of the promise. That is why it is important to take your time and let patience have its perfect work in you. Because we didn't know for ourselves, our engagement was that much harder. We trusted what God told us, but we didn't trust each other because we did not really know each other, and so many issues arose from that.

Whether God reveals to you who your husband is or you have an arranged marriage, I would say find confirming peace within yourself before taking the next step. At the same time, have confidence in what the Lord has spoken. Things do not have to seem perfect. Whatever He has spoken will come to pass, and if He's for you, He is with you and none can be against you.

Are You Willing To Commit?

When you know, the next question is, "Are you willing to commit?" To be honest, this is the chapter at which I am now, while writing this, even though I'm already engaged. Right before the aisle, I'm trying to figure out if I am willing to commit. That's how runaway brides and things like that happen. Those decisions should be taken seriously before engagement, but we get so caught up in the hype of marriage that we skip over it.

I mean, I have committed to this point, through all our ups and downs, but am I willing to go forth one hundred and one percent? I know for myself that he is who I want to be with... but am I willing to work past our problems? Chris is not perfect and neither am I. Am I willing to live with him not being perfect forever?

When you get to the stage of starting to question whether or not you are willing to commit, it is the climax. It is the point of no return. I mean, yes, you can call off the engagement technically, but rightfully, when you say yes to that ring, you are saying yes to more than a ring. You are saying yes to an eternal love, which is what it symbolizes. You are making a promise. Hopefully you are taking that promise and decision seriously. I said yes to the ring without realizing the importance of the decision I was making. Remember, I said yes to the ring twice, with Chris being my second fiancé. I need to be careful, to not practice for divorce.

After the ring, commitment should begin. My decision of commitment now means that from now on, even until after our wedding day, I am committed to Chris no matter what. No matter how bad or good I think he is, for richer or for poorer, in sickness and in health, from now on, I am ready to marry him. Not because I have a million dollars saved, not because I am finished with college, not because things are looking good now, or because I can afford a luxurious wedding, but because I am committed. All these worldly things can pass away and are not strong enough to hold a marriage together. What hold a marriage together are true commitment, faithfulness, and love.

The Process of Engagement

Engagement is a process for me. Though, considering I had an early engagement, many of you may just so happen to encounter this process during courtship. Whatever time it takes place within your relationship before marriage, it MUST take place and you MUST endure it.

During the process, the Lord will continually expose, equip, and encourage you to move forward. This is God working with you and your spouse in order to preserve and strengthen your relationship in Him. When you put God first, you can ensure that the best will come out of your relationship and great things will result not only among you, your spouse, and the Lord, but even between you and the Lord personally.

Success in the process requires obedience, trust, and commitment. You need to be obedient to what the Lord is teaching you and speaking to you during this season. You need to trust in Him and in His word. You need to be committed to the process in order to make it. You can't give up. You need to be willing to be exposed, even to the very depths of you. You need to be willing to be equipped for the battle that the enemy will wage against you because he hates marriages. You need to recognize the little ways in which the Lord will encourage you to press on. Or if you are not meant to be with your spouse, you need to move on. Are you ready?

Family, Family, Family

Another crucial element to consider before saying, "yes" to the ring, as you may have guessed, is family. Have you taken the chance to get to know your spouse's family and even close friends? Yes, you may be marrying one person, but that one person already has many people and things committed to their lives from over time. One of these things just so happens to be, in many cases, family. Usually when a person says yes to the ring, they are saying yes to everything that comes with it. When they say, "I do" for life... that "I do" not only bonds them to their spouse, but also extends that bond to their spouse's family.

I accepted Chris's proposal for engagement an hour before I even knew or met his parents in person. Thank God they turned out to be great people! After proposing to me on Sugar Loaf Mountain, the tallest in Florida, he then drove me to meet his parents for the first time. I guess he had never mentioned much because everything was going too fast. It had only been a little over two months since I had gotten back in touch with him, and I hadn't met his parents from when we were previously dating.

I got to the house and met his parents, and within an hour we announced that we were engaged. Soon, Chris and I were in South Florida, my home. Chris had been preparing to ask my father if I could have his hand in marriage. We were at a family dinner party for my aunt who was in town from Jamaica again, and there were a lot of people over at my Grandmother's house.

When the time came I was so nervous, I started shaking, jittering, and tearing up. Everyone around me knew that something was up. Chris asked my dad if they could take a step outside, and after a few minutes, my dad opened up the front door of the house and he called me outside. He had told me that he accepted Chris's proposal for my hand in marriage and that as long as I am happy, he is happy, under one condition: as long as I finish school and don't start having kids before he's finished having kids himself.

In the middle of my father's acceptance, I broke down crying. I could not believe that this was all going so smoothly, and I thanked God and apologized for worrying so much. Then I showed my father my ring finger that I had been hiding and told him that I already got engaged and laughed, expecting that he would take it like a funny little joke. He seemed pretty cool about it for the rest of the party. He made me call my grandma and aunt out, and we told them what just happened and how Chris and I are engaged, and they hugged us and gave us a few words of encouragement and advice.

Then Chris and I walked into the house and stood there holding hands, and we made the announcement to the whole dinner party. Everyone clapped and was happy. Left and right we were getting congratulated on our engagement. I went to sleep feeling good that night, because everything seemed to have played out perfectly.

The only thing is, once Chris and I were on the way back up to Tallahassee, my Dad kept saying, "Call me when you get home," "We need to talk," and "I need to speak with you; it's important." I figured I was in for something.

When we had our talk, my father expressed to me how he had been losing sleep for the past few days. He did not like the fact that Chris asked him for my hand in marriage after already proposing to me. He said, "There was no point in getting my approval: you guys went off and did what you wanted anyway." Then he started asking me questions about Chris, how we met, how long did we know each other, how do I know I'm ready to get married, and so on. I answered. Then at the end of it all he said, "Promise me this: promise me you won't get married before you finish school."

I said, "Sorry, but I can't promise that, Dad. I love this man, and two years is mad long." "What's the rush?" he said. "What's the wait?" I said. "If I'm ready to be married, I should get married." "How do you know you're ready to be married?" he responded. "I'm not ready to be married; that's why I'm not married now. I'm just ready to be engaged." "If he loves you, he'll wait for you," my father exclaimed. "I know, but I made a vow to God that I would keep my virginity until marriage, and I'm not willing to break that vow because you want me to wait two years to get married. I may not be able to wait that long, and I don't want to wait that long. I love this man, and when I am ready to marry him, I'll marry him." He said, "Ok, well since you made a vow to God, I respect that. Just please take your time and don't rush into anything, and just finish school." "Ok, Dad. Bye."

Long story short, a few months later Chris and I made an announcement to our families that we were going to get married in July. Specifically July 7, 2013. It is July 10, 2013 today, and I am not married. I am simply under my mom's roof, writing this book. I have come to grow a deeper appreciation for my family, though, and for God's timing. We need to just trust in Him and trust that all things are working for our good.

When we made that announcement, alongside the other announcements that I was dropping out of school, moved out of my scholarship house our parents were furious! Especially mine. They thought we were crazy! They all came together—my mom, dad, step dad, and grandma—and had Chris and me meet them at my grandmother's house.

They were most concerned about my survival and well being, they said. They just needed to know how Chris was going to provide for me. They also insisted that I cut this "dropping out of school to start a business" thing and focus on getting my degree rather than focus on getting married.

Then they started to ask us questions about all this "business" and about how Chris planned to provide. It started off as a photography business that I had but since I met Chris, we realized that God gave us complimentary visions to merge into one and extended the business into graphic design and media.

They asked, "Is it incorporated?" "What have you done to start the business, and how do you plan to move it forward?" I responded, "Yes, it is incorporated. The paperwork is all done. I have written out the business plan, and I plan to present it to the School of Business at my University to try to get accepted into their business program as well as applying for their business grants available. If I get accepted into the program, I will have my own office space, and if I get the grant, I will be able to fund my start-up venture." "Why do you want to drop out of school again?" said my step dad.

Chris and I left grandma's house without a resolve and without a contract. Looking back, most of the things they said were true though, and definitely worth thinking about and considering. After praying together, and after being bombarded with phone calls from aunts all around the world the next day encouraging me to stay in school and not make the biggest mistake of my life, Chris and I came to a conclusion.

Our conclusion was, we didn't have a plan, and we needed one. That is one thing we missed from rushing into engagement. We knew what the final result would be because of the visions God had given us about eventually getting married, but we had no idea what would need to take place in between that time. Even though God showed us where we'd eventually end up, it was up to us to get us there. When you are courting, before saying yes to the ring, it is important to find out what your partner's vision and plan for life is. Especially if you are a woman, this is the man who is going to end up leading you. You need to know where you're going, even if God revealed to you that this would be your husband.

If you're wondering why it's important that you have a clear perspective, it's because having a clear perspective will put you in a better position to start on track towards your final goal and not get distracted by other things. Having a clear perspective will cause you to stand firm in obedience to what God is telling you to do when other people come and try to tear your plans down. Having a vision is a part of the foundation that couples need in order to move forward eventually into marriage.

Chris and I prayed, and we finally went to God to help us lay out the plan that we needed in order to bring to pass everything He showed us. We wrote down a list of all the things God was telling us to do. I had my list and Chris had his. We called these lists our "obedience lists". Here is what was on my list:

God has commanded me to:

• Wake up early and spend time with Him every single morning

• Go to sleep by 10:00 pm every night

• Write a business plan and the offical paperwork for IAMImage

• Fast from Facebook and social networks within this season

• Bring a notebook and write everywhere I go

• Memorize all the poems that I have written

• Begin writing my first book, and look for ways to publish it

• Apply for my associates of arts degree

• Fast and pray heavily so that I can be prepared for what lies ahead in my future

• Apply for to FSU's business incubator and grants

• Take P4CM poetry class and audition for Rhetoric

• Focus on cultivating my gifts

• Write down all the prophetic dreams I have and pray to God for revelations on them

• Study with Chris, the purpose and vision of IAMIMAGE and exemplify that

• Learn how to cook an array of various healthy meals

• Refrain from eating meat, fish, and sweets

• Swim and run to get in shape

• Practice obedience and submission towards God and Chris, and trust them to lead

• Cast down vain imaginations during this season of waiting

Our plan was to focus on our lists, step out in faith with the business, and for Chris to get a job temporarily to provide until the business and ministry was developed enough to be our sole source of income. I decided to stay in school, because I could not get into the incubator program without being a student, but to also take the opportunity I have as being a full ride student at my university, to learn all the information I could in order to be a successful writer and business woman.

I decided that if I'm going back to school, I'm doing it for God. I decided to stick with the Creative Writing major and pursue a minor in Psychology and Business.

We called my parents and told them that I would finish school, even though I would not promise that I would not get married until after. We said that Chris would actively seek for a job, and that we would not get married without our parents' honor and blessing.

That happened in March. Now in mid-July, about four and a half months later, here is where I stand as I am writing this:

- I applied for the business program
- I got accepted
- I got the grant
- The business is bringing in more income
- I am writing a book soon to be published
- The business just put a down payment on my first 2-bedroom condo

- I got a new car

Now, God is absolutely amazing! He gave us a step-by-step plan and things are surely coming together because of our obedience. Chris is still looking for a job though. I need to pray for him. Hopefully by the end of this book, a good conclusion of the matter can be written. I am at a standstill. I feel like I am ready to be his wife. I used to pray for Chris all the time, but I fell off because my focus was shifted to so many other things.

Because of how good everything is going, he planned to come down to South Florida this Monday, and we planned to get married in early August just in time to move in to the new place together. I know that Chris is meant to be my future husband, we share the same vision, and I do not believe it is the Lord's will for us to carry them out separately.

All things are possible with God. Go to Him because He has everything and is willing to create anything you need. Others may not be able to see it, but you have to stand in faith, and one day, when it comes to pass, then they'll believe it when they see it.

Finances

Issues with finances can put a real strain on a relationship. When Chris quit his job to pursue an assignment in ministry, I supported him. Now we realize that he needs a job in order to pursue that assignment.

Time and time again in the bible, Jesus performs a spiritual act or a miracle in the lives of those around him, in accordance with natural occurrences or elements. In John 9, for example, when Jesus heals a blind man, He not only did it by spiting in the ground, making mud, and putting it in the man's eyes, but He commanded the man to "wash in the pool of Siloam." This was a miracle. A miracle is a supernatural element and natural element meeting at the same place and time. You know that God is doing something in your life especially when He has spoken a word concerning heavenly things and also given you a command concerning spiritual things, and the environment around you begins to change when you obey. Your environment has been changing because God is working in nature for His glory. Your situation did not start off perfect, but God is perfecting it for His glory, and no one can be given the credit except for Him.

John 9:2-3 (New International Version) says, "And His disciples asked Him, saying, "Rabbi, who sinned, this man or his parents, that he was born blind?" Jesus answered, "Neither this man nor his parents sinned, but that the works of God should be revealed in Him." You may have spent your whole life thinking that God had something against you, while all along, he specifically picked you out to one day manifest Himself to you—to one day prove His glory through you and perform His plan and promise.

I have total confidence that one day the work we do for the Lord will be able to be our sole support; that is my prayer. For now, we have to put in some natural action to get the miracle to come to pass, and that's ok. It's been hard being a bride when I can't pay for anything, but God is faithful, because like I said, only a few days ago I was blessed with a new car and home. Yet in the midst of this season, I've spent nights crying and crying out to Him. I've felt like I'm never going to get married, and I've felt like this wasn't going anywhere. I could not afford anything. When people would ask me, "When's the date?" "When's the date?" I'd sigh or say, "I don't know," or throw out a date that at the time Chris and I had been "standing in faith" on. Trust me, he and I had been standing in faith on a million different dates! Unless you're standing in God's will and timing, standing in faith won't do anything for you!

I was so angry over money that I forgot everything he had done for me when I needed him. Like when he had sacrificed money he had worked long and hard for to pay to get my car fixed. I forgot all the other things he does to show me how much he really loves me.

This whole money thing has made me really wack throughout this engagement, but I am happy that God is renewing my strength. I've been nagging him and tearing him down with my words and reminding him every day that he isn't providing for me. I had to repent and ask the Lord for forgiveness. The Lord told me that He and only He is the ultimate provider. I need to get my focus off of how Chris is not providing for me and get my focus on how God has been providing for us throughout this whole thing. God is faithful! He has not let us down and has been there for us whenever we needed Him, which is always!

I spent middle and high school cheerleading, and now that I am engaged, it's like, where did all my skills of encouragement and good-spiritedness go? Chris grew up as an athlete, a star track player. He understands endurance. My baby is a winner! I knew it when I first met him. There was some sort of light and potential in him, and it was the reason why I was so drawn to him and dropped everyone who I was talking to for him. When did I lose that? When did I start seeing him differently? When money started to clog my perception. Yes, he may be having a hard time right now, but that's temporary.

If you want to get married and you're still in school, I'd recommend going to God and praying about whether it's the right time and in His timing. Find out what His will for your life and your purpose in school are and how you can use it for your marriage and His kingdom. Then you'll have a reason and a confidence as to why you're going through school and the motivation to push through.

Now I know that my education is a tool that I can use for the business and ministry that the Lord is planting through, and it will also be a way to give back to my husband and the family that I am building, and I want them to have the best. Taking care of my education is like me taking care of my household, even now. Every day I desire to be more and more like the proverbs 31 woman.

> "13 She selects wool and flax and works with eager hands. 14 She is like the merchant ships, bringing her food from afar. 15 She gets up while it is still dark; she provides food for her family and portions for her servant girls. 16 She considers a field and buys it; out of her earnings she plants a vineyard. 17 She sets about her work vigorously; her arms are strong for her tasks. 18 She sees that her trading is profitable, and her lamp does not go out at night. 19 In her hand she holds the distaff and grasps the spindle with her fingers."

When you have the time, I suggest that you read the whole passage. Though I just wanted to point out that the proverbs 31 woman was a woman who planned ahead. It said she "gets up while it's still dark," "considers," and "plants." She is a planner and a planter. She realizes that what she does now will come back and bless her family later. It says: "she sees that her trading is profitable." In the same way, I see that my education is profitable spiritually, intellectually, and financially.

As far as finances go, I would also recommend that you and your spouse talk about things like your spending habits, credit scores, credit card debt, and so on because they will definitely have an influence on your financial future. Also, you guys can decide if you feel like one person should be over handling the finances or both. The man doesn't necessarily have to be over organizing the finances just because he's expected to be the provider.

There are a lot of things that you can go over when it comes to finances. Talk about the type of lifestyle that you guys want to live or want to avoid financially. Talk about real estate. Do you prefer renting? Do you prefer buying a house? Do you prefer building a house?

You want to really see where your partner's mindset is at financially. I say mindset because most financial decisions are made off of how someone looks at money. How do you and your spouse view money? Do you view money the same? How does your view of money line up as it relates to the bible?

Spirituality

Earlier in the book, I touched on the importance of being equally yoked with your spouse as well as the importance of getting rid of any unhealthy soul ties. These elements are emphasized because they have the potential to not only hold you back in your relationship with your spouse, but also in your relationship with God.

What you want is to be with someone that will push you closer to God. You want to jointly pursue righteousness with your spouse. You don't want to have to be pulling teeth to drag them along. You don't want open doors for discouragement and doubt within your marriage. You want to glorify God in everything that you do. You want to put God first. That's the most crucial factor to grasp when preparing to enter engagement in the hopes of having a successful marriage: putting God first and keeping God first. Come to think of it, when most people heard our engagement, they admonished us overall to "keep God first." It is so truly important, and it's been the basis of every success that we've had in our engagement thus far and it will be for marriage as well.

When I am speaking about putting God first, I am speaking of putting God first within the season of engagement. In every season you should put God first. Though in engagement, you BOTH should be putting God first, together. If one of you is putting God first and the other is not, it's not going to work. It's just a sign of being unequally yoked.

You may be wondering, "How can I tell whether or not my spouse is putting God first?" The bible says in Matthew 7:16 (New Living Translation), "You can identify them by their fruit, that is, by the way they act. Can you pick grapes from thorn bushes, or figs from thistles?" How does your spouse act, not only towards you, but also towards others? Of course they are not going to be perfect, but are they producing the fruits of the spirit on a consistent basis? Galatians 5:22–23 (New International Version) says: "But the fruit of the Spirit is love, joy, peace, patience, kindness, goodness, faithfulness, gentleness, and self-control. Against such things there is no law." Is your spouse always angry, depressed, complaining, nagging, impatient, rough, etc.?

Not only should you consider the fruit of their works, but what about the fruit of their lips? What are they saying? You can tell a lot about a man's heart by his mouth, because whatever proceeds out of the mouth comes straight from the heart. Do they bring up conversations about the word and the gospel often? Or do they spend most of the time talking about idle and worldly subjects that are of no purpose? Do they spend time gossiping and bashing others? Because if they do, believe me, they will be bashing you behind your back to their friends!

I'm guilty of not exemplifying much fruit either sometimes. If this is you, like it is me, pray this simple prayer with me:

"Lord thank You for sending Your one and only Son, Jesus Christ, to die on the cross for my sins. I believe that Jesus came to bear the sins of the world, died, rose again, and is now seated at Your right hand, and in Him, I have everlasting life. Please change my heart towards You and help my actions and the fruit of my lips line up with this declaration. Take away all the desires within me that are not of You and put your desires in my heart. Tear down all of my idols and take first place in my life. Thank You for it now, Lord, in Jesus' name, Amen."

Communication

Communication is key in every relationship. This was one of the biggest struggles that Chris and I had and are still working on every day by the grace of God. Communication has to do with a lot of things. It deals with more than the fact that you and your spouse should speak to each other about things and relay clear messages back and forth. Communication also deals with the fact that the way you speak to your spouse or relay a message is equally as important.

Are you ready to communicate? In engagement, everything is a "talk," especially if you're doing it God's way and abstaining from sex. Talking will be the only way that you and your spouse can resolve your issues, as keyed off of Mentor and Pastor Cornelius Lindsey, the author of the book So You Wanna Be Married?

When it's time to talk, you can't just walk away from the situation. Depending on who your spouse is, they may interpret walking away as a fear of confronting the problems and issues that you guys may be facing, even to the point of avoiding your own weaknesses. Are you still avoiding your weaknesses? How do you take criticism? These are a few questions you should ask when contemplating your preparedness to communicate.

On the other hand, your spouse may interpret you walking away from the situation as a way to hold in your anger or conceal aggression. The things we do can mean many different things to and for different people. That is why it is up to you to be open about your past, be vulnerable and honest about your fears, and communicate to your spouse. Then, upon that, you both will begin to build up a unified interpretation and understanding of what things mean.

Remember, you are two different people coming from two very different pasts, and many times, from two different backgrounds. In other words, until you communicate, you will be on different pages and have different interpretations that flow from assumptions. Assumptions are the basis of what they call, "a breakdown of communication." That is what our marriage counselor Cornelius would say after Chris and I had an argument: "Oh, y'all just had a breakdown of communication, that's all." As a matter of fact, most of our arguments were a result of a breakdown of communication, and the way we solved them was through communicating.

When I think of a breakdown of communication, I think of a broken-down car. It's all because of the basis of assumption. For example, say you've gone a whole week without intentionally checking the gas meter on your dashboard. On Friday, you just assumed for some odd reason that your gas tank was full, because you hadn't been paying much attention to anything anyway. Then, your car broke down and stopped in the middle of the road because your tank was on "E"! You need to be aware and sensitive to what is going on with your car in order to get places. In the same way, you need to be sensitive and communicate to your spouse in order to move forward in your relationship.

The way you speak to your spouse and the value of the communication that you give is equally as important and will have a significant impact. The way you send a message either kills the message and puts the other person in defensive mode or clearly transmits the message and invites the person to willingly engage in the conversation. When you put gas in your car, you can choose which type of fuel grade you want to use, and whether or not you realize it, it makes a difference in how your car is run. In the same way, the way you and your spouse speak to one another will make a difference in how your relationship is run. It will set the tone, and later on it will even set the tone for the examples your children will follow and how your household is run in the future.

How do you speak to people? Not just in your romantic relationship, but how do you speak to your friends, coworkers, family members, and strangers? Is it consistent across the board, or are you showing favoritism based upon who it is or based upon the situation? You should not show favoritism. Of course it's easier said than done, and I am definitely preaching to myself on this one, but it's important because it's what the bible instructs us to do.

God prepares us for courtship, marriage, engagement, and all these stages of life before we even know it, by His word. Even if never having read my book or never having read any other book on any of these popular relational topics, you can go to God's word for relationship advice. You can also learn from your relationship and encounter with Christ everything that you need to know. With that being said, I am not dogging any Godly counsel or relationship advice; I am just saying you can find it in the word. With everything you learn and all the advice you get, confirm it for yourself with the word, that is, the bible. Do not just take everything at face value. Communicate with your spouse, and you guys decide what works for you and what the spirit of the Lord is telling you to do.

Do you like to nag? Do you like to snap and snap and get on your spouse until you get your way? Well the bible has a lot to say about that. Proverbs 21:9 (New International Version) says, "Better to live on a corner of the roof than share a house with a quarrelsome wife." If you like to nag and quarrel, no one is going to want to be with you! Your spouse might stay with you physically, but emotionally, spiritually, mentally, and verbally, you'll lose them. People may react in different ways, yet in my relationship I know this to be true. When I would nag Chris, he would just shut down. He would hide things from me, not because he had anything to hide, but because he felt like I would judge or criticize him. He would stop thinking logically and start thinking defensively about everything. It's like I turned myself into his enemy. I turned myself against him with my nagging.

Sometimes good communication means keeping your thoughts to yourself and being humble. Sometimes the best communication happens when you're not heard. Communication is always more effective when your actions speak as loud as your words. Are you ready to back up everything that you are claiming to your spouse? Don't you know that when you say yes to the ring, you are saying yes to everything that comes with it, both the good and the bad?

Good communication is measured by word and deed. It is measured by saying more than enough and never too much. It knows when to speak and when to hold the tongue; it knows what to say and how to say it. I can't give you a rulebook or a list of things to say and things not to say. You do this by and through the help of the Holy Spirit. He is that still voice that will lead you. When He's in you and you train yourself to hear Him, through Him and with the word, you will be able to train yourself to communicate lovingly to others.

Pray this prayer with me today...

"Thank You, Lord, for this gift of salvation. Thank You that with this gift, You have promised to give me a comforter. You have promised the Holy Spirit as a guide and a seal to my salvation. Lord, today please baptize me with Your Holy Spirit, strengthen me in my inner man, and put in me the tongues of Your holy language. From this day on, please help me to grow more sensitive to the Holy Spirit living inside of me. Holy Spirit, I pray that You would lead me down the paths of righteousness for Your precious name's sake. In Jesus' name I pray, amen."

Accountability

If you want to be successful at honoring God in your engagement, you have to be willing to accept accountability and be held responsible for your actions. If you are introverted and don't fellowship much with other Christians, you may have to pray about whether it's the right time for you to be engaged. God still probably may want to develop you in certain areas so that when you are engaged, you will be able to use all the tools necessary, one being accountability, to honor Him in the right way.

If you get into engagement as someone who is disengaged from the community, the church, and so on, you are going into engagement unarmed. The enemy now has an opportunity to attack you from each and every way, and if your partner is not strong enough in the faith to lead and pick you up when you fall short, you both will fail miserably. The good news is, where many may be lacking in community, the Holy Spirit can make up for it in conviction.

After Chris got saved, he disconnected from some of his old friends who were associated with his old lifestyle, and he hadn't gotten the chance to really develop new God-fearing friendships with many men when we got engaged. When it comes to me, I have a God-fearing best friend, Damaris, who has been there every second during my engagement, keeping me accountable. I would tell her where we were going, when we were coming back, what we did, what we didn't do, etc.

Still, Damaris is not a whole community. She is just one person. If you have a community of Christian friends, I would recommend that you utilize them for accountability.

Chris and I had to hold each other accountable. We had to set rules and standards and submit to them. God honored that, because for the most part, that worked for us. Yet when we would start to get a little too close, the Holy Spirit would take over EVERY TIME and nothing more would happen. Through this whole journey I've been able to refrain from having sex and/or oral sex with Chris. We have been able to refrain from kissing on the lips. For the first seven months, we didn't kiss at all, after that we started kissing on the cheek. Kissing is not a sin, so we used our discernment and chose when we thought we could handle kissing on the cheek and talked about it. It's been about ten months since we got engaged; God has kept us!

I remember one day when Chris got too close: we were alone in the living room and he was lying on top of me, and right when things were about to get heated... something in him jumped! He jumped right off of me so fast, he grabbed his stuff from the table while I was yelling "FLEE FORNICATION, BABY, FLEE FORNICATION!" and he was out like Speedy Gonzales! I had to run after him to lock the door. That was definitely the Holy Spirit convicting him at that moment; at that time we had to make even stricter rules on ourselves: no late nights in the living room, especially when no one else there.

I am going to be honest. I think that Chris and I have spent more time alone than any other engaged Christian couple I know. I do not recommend this! We've slept under the same roof of our families' houses for over a hundred nights. We've done probably over 60 hours of road-trip driving time together. He could have taken my innocence away if he wanted to. There were times where I wanted to be with him so bad and I said seductive things I shouldn't have said, and he'd tell me to stop and he'd leave the room. He had the chance. He could have taken advantage of me, but he never did. He always held me accountable.

Now, I mentioned before that Chris didn't get to develop any new God-fearing friendships, but there was an exception. When Chris and I first got engaged, the thought crossed my mind, "whose going to keep him accountable?" Then I felt led by the Holy Spirit to message Pastor Cornelius Lindsey online and tell him about my fiancé and our situation. No longer than a day later he responded and had me connect them both through email. They set up a day where they talked over the phone, but before they did, during my conversation with Chris, I explained to him, "Remember when we were first together and I came up with all these standards like no kissing or coming to my house and I started to respect myself? Well the guy you are about to talk to, he and his wife are the ones who inspired me to do that. I've been listening to his sermons and reading her blogs, and that is what inspired me to make that change." Chris's response: "What?! That's who I am going to speak to? This man changed my life..."

A few minutes later they were on the phone speaking. A few weeks later Chris and I met Cornelius and Heather Lindsey at a speaking engagement in Gainesville, Fl., two hours away from Tallahassee. Soon they became our friends and our marriage counselors; they have been there for us throughout this whole thing, both spiritually and financially, and I can't be any more grateful. Around the same time they needed graphic designers, and Chris and I both had the skills needed to assist them in their needs, and it is a great pleasure to do so! My business started off as a photography business. They are the ones who inspired us to consider extending it out to web design and graphics. I thank God for this Godly connection and awesome source of accountability. Now that I think about it, I may not have a big group of close friends to keep me accountable, but all my Pinky Promise ladies and the Pinky Promise movement have been there for me from the beginning. Pinky Promise is what got me on the right path and what is helping me keep it until marriage.

Look around you. God may be putting different forms of accountability in your life, and you don't even know it. It's not until now, when I am writing, that I have realized how much Pinky Promise and Heather's emails and Cornelius's bed checks have really kept me in check. Thank God for this ministry!

You are going to be tempted, and you have to know how to deal with that. I will give you three passages of scripture that I have stood upon during my engagement that helped me to resist the temptation.

James 1:13–14 (New International Version): "When tempted, no one should say, 'God is tempting me.' For God cannot be tempted by evil, nor does he tempt anyone; but each person is tempted when they are dragged away by their own evil desire and enticed."

1 Corinthians 10:13 (New International Version): "No temptation has overtaken you except what is common to mankind. And God is faithful; he will not let you be tempted beyond what you can bear. But when you are tempted, he will also provide a way out so that you can endure it."

Ephesians 6:12–18 (New International Version): "12 For our struggle is not against flesh and blood, but against the rulers, against the authorities, against the powers of this dark world and against the spiritual forces of evil in the heavenly realms. 13 Therefore put on the full armor of God, so that when the day of evil comes, you may be able to stand your ground, and after you have done everything, to stand. 14 Stand firm then, with the belt of truth buckled around your waist, with the breastplate of righteousness in place, 15 and with your feet fitted with the readiness that comes from the gospel of peace. 16 In addition to all this, take up the shield of faith, with which you can extinguish all the flaming arrows of the evil one. 17 Take the helmet of salvation and the sword of the Spirit, which is the word of God. 18 And pray in the Spirit on all occasions with all kinds of prayers and requests. With this in mind, be alert and always keep on praying for all the saints."

If you are currently in a season where it seems like temptation is all around you, I recommend that you write down the previous bible verses on index cards, or ones similar to them, and take them with you! Pull them right out and read them as a way of escape during those tempting moments!

I would recommend joining the following movements:

Pinky Promise (for women):

http://www.pinkypromisemovement.com

The Oath (for men):

http://www.theoathmovement.com

Being Stripped by God

So, you've been hearing me refer to engagement as a process and you may be wondering, what do I mean by this process? Well, within the season of engagement, God has a way of stripping you of things that are not like Him, even right before the eyes of your spouse. You have to understand, this is not a physical stripping—this is a spiritual stripping that your spouse will be able to recognize if they are in tune with the Holy Spirit.

All the things that the Lord will reveal to you during this time will be things that you and your spouse have to work on during your season of engagement. Some things will be pertinent to get solved before you get married, and some things you will have to continue working on even during marriage. To measure the difference, you simply have to be led by the Holy Spirit.

Something that God stripped Chris of was his distrust towards me. Like stated previously, the fact that he did not trust me raised up a lot of issues and arguments during our engagement. The Holy Spirit brought this to the forefront, and we had to work towards building up trust between one another. Now that he does trust me, our relationship has been running a lot more smoothly and we're closer to getting married.

Something that God is stripping me of and He will continue stripping me of even after Chris and I get married is my mouth. God has been helping me every day to learn how to keep it shut when I don't need to say anything and open it wide when Chris needs me the most. Words have the power of life and death in them. Every day God has been helping me to become more submissive and supportive towards Chris, yet this is not something that can just change over night. It is a matter of dying to myself for my spouse daily. For the rest of my life, everyday that I wake up, I have to commit myself to living a life of love and humility and honoring my husband, because that honors God.

Being stripped by God is amazing. It's an indicator that He is with you and that He is working on you and on your relationship. Be careful, though: you need to distinguish the difference between whether God is revealing things to you to help you, warn you, or both. Sometimes God is simply just showing you someone's true colors so that you can leave that relationship!

I knew that God was both helping me and warning me for my benefit and for the betterment of my relationship. When something would come up with Chris that I would not know how to deal with, or when we'd get into a big argument... I would go to the Lord in prayer. I would say, "Lord, is this the man that you really want me to be with? If so, please show me how to deal with him and this situation. If not, please take this man out of my life." When you pray those types of prayers, whatever follows after will show you what the Lord is doing and whether you're meant to be with that person. Whenever I prayed that prayer for Chris, God always led me with what to do, and shortly after, the situation would be resolved.

Now, the Lord didn't always tell me what I wanted to hear. Sometimes He'd be like, "Go apologize for speaking back to him," and I'd be like, "What! But he was wrong. He gets on my nerves, Daddy!" then after my little tantrum I'd go apologize because I knew that if God was helping me, Chris was meant to be my husband, and I was willing to do what it took to make it work.

Engagement and being stripped by God are not easy, but they are definitely a process to appreciate while preparing for the stage of marriage. All I've got to say is commit to the process! Don't cut the process short like a bad perm. Let the Lord complete His full work in your relationship during the season before saying, "I do."

Sacrificing and Dying to Self

We talked about it for a little bit, but I want to go deeper into what "sacrificing and dying to self" means. Firstly, I want to speak about sacrificing. Are you willing to sacrifice your time and attention to focus on your engagement, or are you at a season in life where you can't make that type of adjustment? When I made the decision to get engaged, a lot of other things got put on hold or were even completely deleted from my life; one of them being a lot of friends I used to have.

When you enter into a relationship with someone you are becoming one with, anyone else who becomes a threat to that oneness needs to go. If you are a female with a lot of male friends or if you are a male with a lot of female friends, depending on your spouse's personality, be ready for the dynamic of your relationships with the opposite sex to be altered and changed. Lawrence and Cle were like big brothers to me, and they still are. Still, though, I can't go with Bestie and sleep over at their house like we used to. Even if it's just innocent fun, I have to be cautious of how things look, especially now. I can't leave any room for the enemy, and I especially don't want to leave room for Chris to lose trust in me again. I had a guy that I called my best friend, and we were really close. He was my prayer partner as well as business partner, but as I made the sacrifice to draw closer to my fiancé, Chris began taking the position of all those places in my life.

It's ok to start off friends with people from the opposite sex. It's not a sin. That is how many of us develop in a relationship and get to know our spouses in the beginning. Yet make sure that every friendship you have with someone of the opposite sex eventually becomes intentional, or else it'll eventually become something else. Later on, you have to be willing to face the fact that the dynamic of your relationship with others may have to change when your spouse is in the picture. I am not saying that you should change or become "brand new". I'm just saying that the way you fellowship with others should change. Whether you distance yourself a little or you bring your spouse into the picture, you can choose which way best fits when it comes to dealing with relationships that began in the past.

I've seen people who have had friends of the opposite sex when they get into a relationship. Instead of drifting away, like I said, they bring their friends together with their spouse, and now it's like a big comfortable group. This all depends on the type of personality your spouse has and how they feel about it. If you already gave your spouse a reason not to trust you, this technique may not be the best. You probably need to just drift away a little, and explain to whoever needs explaining why. This is a sensitive area, so of course pray and let the Holy Spirit lead you on this one.

In marriage you will have to make a lot of sacrifices, and practicing for this begins with engagement. Engagement leads to marriage, so if you are saying that you are ready to be engaged, you are saying that when the time comes, you are ready to sacrifice whatever it may be for your marriage. Are you sure it's your time? Or are you still 100% committed to what you are doing now?

I am not saying that being committed to something and being single is wrong. For instance, I admire people who spend years in medical school or years in ministry building up and preparing to make a way for their future families. There is nothing wrong with that. There is also nothing wrong with meeting your spouse while you are in the middle of something. God may be sending them to help you finish that thing! Chris is helping me to do God's work. We work together. At the end of the day, it's all about God's timing.

It is the heart of a true husband is to lay down his life for his bride. It is the heart of Christ. Ephesians 5:25 says: "Husbands, love your wives, just as Christ loved the church and gave himself up for her." The Lord commands our husbands to follow Christ's example, but also like the Church should submit to Christ, the wife should submit to the husband. She should die to herself. She should abandon her own selfish desires and follow the leadership of her head, which comes from God. She becomes one with her husband. In Galatians 2:20, the apostle Paul proclaims, "I have been crucified with Christ. It is no longer I who live, but Christ who lives in me. And the life I now live in the flesh I live by faith in the Son of God, who loved me and gave himself for me." This takes obedience. If you are obedient to God, you will not have a hard time being obedient to your husband, because though your husband is the head of you, the head of him is Christ and

then the Father. So you want to be engaged? Are you obedient
to God?

A Concluding Letter

How then do you know if you are ready to enter any stage of life? Whether it is courtship, engagement, marriage, college, a new job, a new place, or whatever it may be, one of the most important things to consider is the timing. God has made everything beautiful in its time.

If you want to trust in God's timing, you need faith. He is an eternal God, which means that all things in Him already exist before they manifest or come to life on earth, or before what one would consider to be "God's timing." God's true timing was then, is now, and forever more. When your spiritual faith is met with a natural opportunity that is presented by God, then things are working in His timing. He is in control of the timing because He creates the opportunity; all you have to do is hope in Him and step out in faith.

For example, I began waiting on God's timing to marry Chris. I had the faith; I knew that when God brought the opportunity in line with my faith, then it would be the time. I had an opportunity to get a home, I applied and believed God for it, and I got it. Chris and I then had a place to move in to, which opened up the opportunity for us to marry, so we did.

I am now writing this conclusion as a married woman! I wrote this book while I was engaged and by the grace of God I am publishing it as Karolyne Roberts. This book was a search for answers to many questions I had, and it was also an opportunity for God to answer them. This makes it His perfect timing. There are many things that exist for you, but you are waiting on God's timing. God's timing happens when you step out in faith. God timing happens when you are obedient to His calling.

You only know for sure if it was God's timing, at the end of the thing. If it truly was God's timing, what you stepped out in faith for, will then be confirmed and completed beautifully. Now, when you step out, things won't necessarily be perfect. That's the point. You have to trust Him.

Chris and I did not have a big wedding and no, everything was not how I always dreamed. I can honestly say though, everything God has brought us through is above and beyond what I could ever ask for or even think of. I trusted God. Even though Chris and I hardly had anything when we decided to take the big step, that is, anything materialistic, we had each other. We had faith.

Shortly after, everything began coming together smoothly. God began to bring people and family members to pour into our lives. I do not regret for one second making the decision to be Christopher Roberts' wife. He prays with me, laughs with me, cries with me—he's so perfect for me. God has made him so strong and prepared him so well for this role. I am so excited for the journey ahead of us. Despite what people say or think, we are happy at the end of the day, and we have God here with us, all along the way.

Made in the USA
San Bernardino, CA
03 May 2015